Three Mysteries Revealed

Three Mysteries Revealed

Three Books in One

Dr. James B. Reesor

VANTAGE PRESS
New York

Published by Vantage Press, Inc.
516 West 34th Street, New York, New York 10001

Manufactured in the United States of America
ISBN: 0-533-13412-9

Library of Congress Catalog Card No.: 99-97535

0 9 8 7 6 5 4 3 2 1

For the encouragement, assistance, and prayers of my wife, Mary, our three children, James, Jeanette, and Yvonne, our assistants, partners, friends, and relatives, I lovingly dedicate this book.

It is our earnest prayer that the scriptural contents of the book will make a lasting and productive impact upon their lives.

Contents

Three Mysteries Revealed

God's Grand Redemptive Design
Dr. James B. Reesor
and
Professor John H. Goodyear III

Foreword

Those of us who have observed and participated in the widespread ministry of Dr. James B. Reesor know that the gravity and humility with which he perceives his mission, to take the gospel into all the world, is genuine and selfless. If there is one Scripture that can focus succinctly on Rev. Reesor's consummate desire, it is John 3:30: "He (the Lord Jesus Christ) must increase, but I must decrease."

This spirit of dedication and determination to give only his best for the Master's service in evangelizing, discipling, teaching, and writing is a lifestyle for all believers to follow. Paul encourages New Testament Christians to follow him as he follows Christ; Brother Reesor would echo that admonition.

After sixty years or more of laboring in the harvest fields, Dr. Reesor continues to look to the future with an "eye of timelessness." Thus it is fitting that this book would focus on GOD'S GRAND REDEMPTIVE DESIGN, seeking to have all believers understand that nothing short of a perfect, pure, and holy relationship will exist between God the Father, God the Son, and God the Holy Spirit, the faithful angels, and redeemed mankind—FOREVER.

For me to have a part of this project of proclaiming the eternal good news, is a privilege indeed.

J.H. Goodyear III, Ph.D.

Introduction

The motivation for the printing of this book on God's Total Redemptive Design was provided to me over a period of years. First of all by questions presented by inquisitive minds, while I was serving as President of the International Bible College located in Moose Jaw, Saskatchewan, Canada, and then later by those who attended our meetings, when I was conducting special prophetic revivals, and teaching from a large chart.

Each lecture period ended with a question-and-answer period. Much prayer, research, and concentrated study was required in providing biblical answers. When it was impossible to provide an instant biblical answer, we suggested a postponement until such a time as the Holy Spirit provided additional spiritual illumination.

Then too, it was our desire to present truth in a manner that would appeal to all individuals, young and older. With this prayer in mind, I solicited the able assistance of Professor John H. Goodyear III to assist with the work of compiling scriptural material and presenting it in an orderly, Bible study outline. It is our prayerful desire that this presentation may serve to develop a more unified relationship between truth-seeking, spiritually hungry, sincere believers. God's plan from the past eternity is unfolding more and more as He prepares His people for life in the future eternity.

To be sure, the Creator of the universe, and all good things therein, were first of all provided for His righteous angelic beings, in their different orders. Then man was created to succeed the fallen angels in the plan of God. Yet, because the triune God made us with an inviolate freedom to choose, He took a "risk," which would allow the possibility of the wrong choice to be made. No interruption of God's perfect design would have occurred had man obeyed, but because of sin, He deemed His redemptive plan to be necessary. Tragically, however, the disobedient choice was made and sin has severed an otherwise holy and perfect relationship. To repair the "break" and restore our relationship requires the redemption of each inherently sinful person born to mankind. The degeneration of all aspects of planet earth and its inhabitants is, as a result, presently "groaning and awaiting" (Rom. 8:22) a complete regeneration provided by our Redeemer, Jesus Christ!!!

Yes, we are living in the "present" eternity, but God chose to call this part of eternity "time." Time is simply a fragment of eternity reduced to a period of 7000 years, seven of God's days, in which the Lord is in the process of fulfilling His plan of total redemption.

Time began, as we understand it, the hour of man's disobedient act in the Garden of Eden, and time as we reckon it will be no more when we are ushered onto the New Earth. Yes, time is a measure of change, and during each segment of time, major events have transpired on earth. We may refer to these segments as periods of Divine Administration.

We are presenting four aspects of God's Grand Redemptive Design, and these four divisions provide outline material for four separate seminars, sermons or studies. They are as follows:

1. The Purpose and Need for Redemption
2. The Power and Cost of Redemption
3. The Promise and Provision for Redemption
4. The Rewards and Responsibilities of Redemption

Each of the four sections focuses on an explanation of that aspect, as an integral part of God's Grand Design, appropriately followed by questions and suggestions for further study and discussion.

Total redemption, as presented in the Bible, reveals that every good thing provided by our beneficent Heavenly Father, in the Garden of Eden, will be restored to His redeemed sons and daughters.

If our God, in His infinite knowledge and wisdom, would choose to provide us with glimpses into the future life, and thus give us a preview of His eternal kingdom, when His redeemed sons and daughters are enjoying that glorious, utopian, and harmonious lifestyle, many more would receive salvation.

However, it is the will of God that we receive salvation by faith, and then proceed to render unto God the love, worship, and obedience that he has every right to expect. Just as Adam's act of willful disobedience resulted in broken fellowship and death, so likewise our acts of disobedience may also sever our fellowship with God, and require genuine repentance to experience renewal and restoration.

The reality of the future life in our Lord's eternal kingdom will be so much greater than our most vivid imagination or comprehension in this present life, that there is no comparison.

If sinners could have one glimpse of heaven, and the glorious future life of joy, peace, happiness, and glory, their lives would be revolutionized. Why not believe God, and His word, accepting it by faith, for "Faith comes by hearing and hearing by the Word of God" (Romans 10:17).

Let's examine His Grand Design with excitement, anticipation, and thankfulness.

The Purpose and Need for Redemption

Redemption Defined:

Total redemption involves the full restoration of every good thing God provided in creation. It includes "the recovery of that which was mortgaged or pledged; the payment of a debt or obligation" (Dictionary definition).

God's plan is perfect, from the very beginning of creation somewhere in the eternal past, on through this 7000-year period we know as time, and on into that never-ending eternal future.

The Bible says, "For My thoughts are not your thoughts, neither are your ways My ways, saith the Lord. For as the heavens are higher than the earth, so are My ways higher than your ways, and My thoughts than your thoughts" (Isaiah 55:8,9).

Many ask the question: "Why does man require redemption?" When God created man, male and female, He made them righteous, in His own image and likeness. He made them immortal beings, with bodies consisting of flesh, blood and bones. If they had not sinned, they would have lived eternally in their incorruptible bodies, according to God's perfect plan.

God's Son, Co-Creator with the Father and Holy Spirit from the beginning, pleased His Father so perfectly that the Father desired myriads of sons and daughters to worship and fellowship with Him eternally. Therefore, He commanded man in the Garden of Eden, in their immortal state, to multiply and replenish the earth, as the Bible tells us. What plan could be more perfect?

9

Our understanding is presently limited, but in the future life, we will understand all things.

"So God created man in His own image, in the image of God created He him, male and female created He them. And God blessed them, and God said unto them, Be fruitful, and multiply, and replenish the earth (repopulate) and subdue it: and have domination over the fish of the sea, and over the fowl of the air, and over every living thing that moveth upon the earth" (Genesis 1:27,28).

The Bible does not reveal the length of man's life in the Garden of Eden, from the hour of his creation to the time of his fall. The Scriptures indicate that he lived long enough to obey the command of God and begin the work of reproduction. Children born during the period of Innocence were born in righteousness. It is believed by many that the "sons of God" referred to in Genesis 6:1–7 were children born to Adam and his wife in the Garden of Eden, prior to the Fall. Cain and Abel were the first two children born after the Fall.

After Cain murdered his brother Abel, he went to the land of Nod. The Bible says: "And Cain went out from the presence of the Lord, and dwelt in the land of Nod, on the east of Eden. And Cain knew his wife; and she conceived, and bare Enoch: and he builded a city, and called the name of the city, after the name of his son, Enoch" (Gen. 4:16,17). Did Cain build a city for one wife and one son?

God instituted a law when He placed man in the Garden of Eden. He said, "Of every tree of the garden you may freely eat: But of the tree of knowledge of good and evil, you may not eat of it: for the day that you eat thereof you shall surely die" (Gen. 2:16,17).

Eve was deceived by the devil, who approached her in the form of the serpent, lied to her and led her to believe that she would not die, but would receive greater knowledge. She ate of the fruit and gave to Adam, so they both sinned.

Their sinful act affected their offspring, including those also who were born prior to the Fall, as the Word says, "Nevertheless death reigned from Adam to Moses, even over them that HAD NOT SINNED after the similitude of Adam's transgression, . . ." (Romans 2:16,17). Why is this age-old topic so vital to our understanding as we enter the twenty-first century? What is the problem?

In the Garden of Eden, man mortgaged his soul to satan, along with the entire dominion God had entrusted to him. Sin abounded on every hand. Lucifer had rebelled against God and had led his third of the angels in rebellion. They were defeated by Michael and Gabriel and their righteous angels, it is believed, so Lucifer became the adversary, satan, the god of this world, and his angels became fallen angels. So satan, the god of this world, is leading unbelievers on the broad way that leads to hell and the lake of fire.

The Bible says, "But if our Gospel be hid, it is hid to them that are lost: in whom the god of this world has blinded the minds of them that believe not, lest the light of the glorious Gospel of Christ, who is the image of God, should shine unto them" (2 Corinthians 4:3,4).

America's post-Christian culture has embraced false, deceptive, and destructive teaching promoted by atheists, communists, modernists, and the so-called New Age focus, rejecting the Bible as being the inspired, inerrant Word of God. Fulfilled prophecy, as recorded in the Bible, provides adequate evidence of the inerrancy of God's Word to satisfy souls who are hungry for Truth. Jesus said, "I am the Way, the Truth, and the Life" (John 14:a).

Man in his debased, deceived, and sinful state is certainly in need of a Redeemer, and Jesus Christ, God the Son, became our Savior. Through His substitutionary death, as "The Lamb slain from the foundation of the world" (Revelation 13:8b), and "It, (the Seed of the woman) shall bruise thy head, and thou shalt bruise his heel" (Genesis 3:15b), we have redemption.

Jesus came to set the captives free, to break every yoke, and to pay off the mortgage in full. He came to destroy the works of the devil, as the Bible says: "That He might destroy the works of the devil" (1 John 3:8d).

Only Christ Jesus our Lord and Redeemer has the power and the authority to forgive our sin and cleanse us from its power and bondage. False religions can never satisfy the inherent hunger of the soul.

The poison of sin entered our bloodstream because of Adam's sin and all of his descendants inherited the sinful nature. The result of sin was sickness, disease and death. Man lost his immortality and down through the centuries has been forced to live in a mortal, corruptible body. His only hope of a total restoration is through the grand redemptive plan that was finished when our Lord Jesus hung suspended on a cruel cross and declared, "It is finished." He died and poured forth His precious blood to redeem us from sin.

The Word tells us: "For if the blood of bulls and of goats, and the ashes of an heifer sprinkling the unclean, sanctifieth to the purifying of the flesh: How much more shall the blood of Christ, who through the eternal Spirit offered Himself to God, purge your conscience from dead works to serve the living God?" (Hebrews 9:13,14).

The Apostle Paul also expressed the work of redemption very well when he said, "But of Him are you in Christ Jesus, who became for us wisdom from God and righteousness and sanctification and redemption, that as it is written, He who glories, let him glory in the Lord" (1 Corinthians 1:30,31).

The inspired Word also tells us: "For He made Him who knew no sin to be sin for us, that we might be made the righteousness of God in Him" (2 Corinthians 5:21).

That which was lost through Adam's sin was regained through the sacrificial ministry of Jesus. "And so it is written, The first man Adam was made a living soul; the last Adam was made a quickening Spirit" (1 Corinthians 15:45).

We are therefore, "Being justified freely by His grace

through redemption that is in Christ Jesus" (Romans 3:24). We died with Christ two thousand years ago because He died in our place that we may live with Him eternally.

Study: Focus Questions and Answers

QUESTION: Why does mankind need redemption?
ANSWER: Romans 5:12–18 gives the most succinct reason:

> Therefore, as by one man sin entered into the world, and death by sin, so death passed onto all men, for all have sinned. (V12) Nevertheless, death reigned from Adam to Moses, even over those who had not sinned in the similitude of Adam's transgression, he being the figure of Him who was to come. (V14) For if by one man's offense death reigned by one, much more those who receive abundance of grace and the gift of righteousness shall reign in life by One, Jesus Christ. (V17) Therefore as by the offense of one, judgement to condemnation came upon all men, even so by the righteousness of One, the free gift unto justification of life came upon all men. For as by one man's disobedience many were made sinners, so by the obedience of One shall many be made righteous," (V18 & 19) (21Kj)

QUESTION: Don't the major religions of the world each provide a path for mankind to find purpose, meaning, as "believers" seek the Creator God? Isn't each similar in its "design" of purpose—to relate to God?
ANSWER: In brief, Orthodox Jews follow the Law of Moses and live a moral lifestyle based on Old Testament guidelines detailing a relationship with Jehovah God, still awaiting the "promised Messiah." Muslims commit to service based on the "Five Pillars of Islam," pray five times daily, fast, and make a pilgrimage to Mecca, in an effort to relate favorably to Allah.

Hindus seek good "Karma" by going through a series of reincarnations, attempting to live ethically, and to immerse themselves into the divine.

Buddhists work untiringly to erase desire and arrive at the "nothingness" of Nirvana after many reincarnated lives. These world religions have obvious commonalities; that fundamental element is seen in man seeking God.

Christianity, in stark contrast, is not really a "religion" as much as it is a relationship in which Creator God is seeking out His special creation—mankind—with the good news of redemption. God's Grand redemptive Design is for whosoever will (John 3:16&17) and is effected through the miracle of God entering human history in the Person of Jesus Christ, who provided the sacrifice for man's inherent sinful nature.

Consequently, "There is no other name under heaven whereby man can be saved. . . ." (Acts 4:12) "For by grace are ye saved through faith; and that not of yourselves: it is the gift of God: Not of works, lest any man should boast" (Ephesians 2:8&9).

In short, DOING (works as seen in man's religious instruction) will not replace BEING (relationship relating to Father God as a redeemed son/daughter—bought by blood of the Son).

The Power and Cost of Redemption

Much publicity pertaining to vast displays of power has influenced large segments of humanity to believe that man is quite capable of deciding his own destiny, apart from God. We are aware of nuclear power, political power, electrical power, mechanical power, medical power, people power, and a great variety of other demonstrations of power, many good and many evil.

As Christians we have learned to recognize and appreciate divine power, for without God's power, we would not be here. Certainly, God's creative and sustaining power is so far beyond man's united efforts to invent and manufacture various areas of power, that the greatest human minds are utterly incapable of comprehending the unlimited sources of GOD POWER.

The Bible speaks to us, over and over, and over again of God's omnipotent power. For example: "In the beginning was the Word, and the Word was with God, and the Word was God. The same was in the beginning with God. All things were made by Him; and without Him was not anything made that was made. In Him was life; and the life was the light of men" (John 1:1–4).

The evolutionist chooses to reject God from his thinking, so he accepts satan's lie and believes the stupid theory of evolution. Yes, that is certainly what it is: merely a stupid theory. True scientists tell us it is an absolute impossibility, but gullible souls, who love darkness rather than light, have gobbled up the lie and devote their time trying to convince others to do likewise.

They remind us of the ape with a copy of the Bible in one hand and a copy of Darwin's book, *The Origin of the Species* in the

15

other hand, trying to decide whether he was his brother's keeper or his keeper's brother.

Can you possibly imagine a mosquito evolving into an elephant? If so, where did the mosquito come from?

The Apostle Peter correctly prophesied of scoffers who would appear in the last days. He said: "That you may be mindful of the words that were spoken before by the Holy Prophets, and of the commandment of us the Apostles of the Lord and Savior:

"Knowing this first, that there shall come in the last days scoffers, walking after their own lusts, And saying, 'Where is the promise of His coming? For since the fathers fell asleep, all things continue as they were from the beginning of creation' " (2 Peter 3:2–4, KJV).

Scoffers, walking after their own lusts, are easily led into deception, and so accept false teachings and false religions, including the ridiculous theory of evolution. Teachers of evolution take their students back billions of years to nothing, and then in their weird imagination endeavor to evolve all forms, varieties, and species of life out of nothing. Such stupidity can only result in their own eternal damnation.

These poor, deluded creatures, with their closed minds, accuse Christians of being narrow minded, ignorant, using their faith as a crutch, an escape hatch. Man is categorized with the animal kingdom, a descendant of the ape, and sad to say, many of them act worse than animals. Christians, to say the least, have a great advantage over the religion of the evolutionist. The evolutionist does not know who he is, where he came from, why he is here, or where he is going.

As Christians, we know our origin, our composition, the purpose of our existence, and our eternal destiny. We do not hate the evolutionist, but rather feel sorry for him. As Christians, we love them, pray for them, and desire to lead them to Christ, but we despise their teachings, which are of satanic origin.

Christ Jesus came to lead sincere people from darkness into

light, from confusion into a living, active faith in God. This also is our mission.

The total cost of our redemption is impossible for us to comprehend with our finite minds. It far exceeds our human ability to grasp the significance of the price our Lord paid, in physical sacrifice alone, but the actual cost extends far beyond the mental and bodily anguish that He endured, that we may experience His total redemption.

As God and Co-Creator of all good things, from the very beginning of creation in the eternal past, we are made to realize that we belong to Him first of all by right of creation.

When man was created in the Garden of Eden, God gave him dominion over the earth and everything on it. But, when man sinned, he mortgaged himself and the entire planet to satan and after being driven out of the garden, he was compelled to face the future living under the curse of God.

However, because Jesus as Co-Creator of the earth, and thus part owner of the earth and all that He had created, He was willing to become a curse for us, as the Bible says: "For it is written, Cursed is everyone that hangeth on a tree" (Gal. 3:13b).

Under the law, when a piece of property was mortgaged, the original owner was permitted to redeem it. Therefore, as original owner, Jesus was authorized to fulfil the work of redemption. As He hung suspended upon the cruel cross, with the thorns of the thorny crown piercing his scalp, His sacred body wracked with pain, He cried out in anguish, "It is finished." Forsaken as He was, by God and man, He bore our sins past, present, and future, in His own body, and poured forth His life's blood to cleanse us from all sin. He paid the mortgage in full, to deliver redeemed souls from every curse, and prepare for us a kingdom that shall never end.

The very least we can do is to say: "Lord, I belong to you first of all by right of creation and now also by right of redemption. Take my life and use it to your glory."

You may have noticed that certain other translators have

omitted certain words, sentences, and even verses from their versions, as compared to the original KJV, to suit their particular brand or theology. Prominent and reliable Bible scholars agree that the regular KJV is the most authentic Bible in print.

The work of redemption incorporates all divine attributes in a determined effort to undo the havoc wrought in the human family by evil, destructive powers, under the leadership of satan, the fallen angels, demonic spirits, and wicked people.

God, in His omnipotent, omniscient, and omnipresent power, is successfully accomplishing His redemptive work in spite of opposition from satan and all the united forces of evil. Jesus said, "Upon this Rock I will build my Church and the gates of hell shall not prevail against it." Jesus is the Rock that He referred to, and unless the Church is built on Him, it cannot stand.

Gullible, unstable souls, unwilling to submit to the will of God, and His precious Word, have wallowed in the slime pits of sin, opening their minds and hearts to deception, and are speeding down the broad and slippery route that leads to a never-ending hell and lake of fire.

Jesus said, "I am the Way, the Truth, and the Life: no man cometh unto the Father, but by Me" (John 14:6). Without Him there is no going, there is no knowing, and there is no genuine living. He came that we may have life and that more abundantly, as He said (John 10:10). Through the simple expediency of believing God and putting our faith and personal choice into action, we are saved.

Jesus told Martha, the sister of Lazarus, on the occasion of the death of Lazarus: "I am the resurrection, and the life: he that believeth in Me, though he were dead, yet shall he live: And whosoever liveth and believeth in Me shall never die. . . ." (John 11:25,26).

The Scriptures indicate that the original earth, the pre-Adamic age, was inhabited by nations of angelic beings, of whom Lucifer was their king. One important reference concerning this past state of habitation, on the part of angelic beings is Isaiah 14:12–15, which reads:

> How art thou fallen from heaven, O Lucifer, son of the morning! How art thou cut down to the ground, which did'st weaken the nations! For thou hast said in thine heart, I will ASCEND INTO HEAVEN, I will EXALT MY THRONE above the stars of God: I will sit also upon the mount of the congregation, in the sides of the north: I will ascent ABOVE THE HEIGHTS OF THE CLOUDS; I will be like the most High. Yet thou shalt be brought down to hell, to the sides of the pit.

God cursed the earth because of Lucifer's rebellion, and the earth was left in a state of gross darkness, causing the death to all forms of life, and entered the ice age. Many of the mammoth animals that roamed over the earth in its original state became extinct. The angels who followed Lucifer in his rebellion became fallen angels. In His time God decided to restore the earth and He accomplished the work of re-creation. It has been suggested that God created man to succeed Lucifer and have dominion over the earth.

When God created man, He commanded him to multiply and "replenish" the earth (Genesis 1:28). This word is used in the regular KJV, and it means to "REPOPULATE." Most other translations have omitted the word from their versions. The word is translated from the Hebrew word "MALE," pronounced "MAW-LAY" or "MALA," meaning to fill, to be full, accomplish, replenish. The same word is used in Genesis 9:1, when God commanded Noah and his family to be "fruitful, multiply and replenish the earth."

Much confusion has resulted from different translations, when the translators relied on their human intellect in providing different versions that do not harmonize with the regular KJV.

Through the process of God's Grand Redemptive Design, His redeemed sons and daughters will possess bodies similar to the bodies of our foreparents in the Garden of Eden, consisting of flesh, blood, and bones. Otherwise, God would have accomplished only a partial redemption.

At the time of the rapture for the living saints, and the resurrection of the righteous believers who have been promoted from this present life, our bodies will be instantly changed from mortality to immortality, from corruption to incorruption, and we shall live eternally in the prime of life.

If you have experienced this redemptive work in your life, and are learning to "live and walk in the Spirit," as He tells us in Galatians 5:25, you are being qualified by the love, mercy, and grace of God to occupy positions of honor and responsibility in His future, eternal kingdom. May I remind you that gold, silver, precious gems, and all of the united wealth of the world could never purchase our salvation. We could never earn it, pay for it, or be good enough within ourselves to deserve it, for "By grace we are saved through faith; and that not of ourselves: it is the gift of God" (Ephesians 2:8).

By faith we receive this wonderful, soul-cleansing power that brings us into a personal relationship with our Lord Jesus Christ, for "As many as received Him, to them gave He power to become the sons of God, even to them that believe on His Name" (John 1:12).

Oceans of water can never cleanse us from sin, all of the cleansing agencies on earth can never cleanse us from sin, good works can never cleanse us from sin, pagan and modern religions can never cleanse us from sin, but, PRAISE THE LORD! The pure blood of our Lord Jesus Christ, through the everlasting Covenant, not only cleanses us from sin but keeps us pure and righteous, through faith in His finished work of redemption.

Study: Focus—Questions and Answers

QUESTION: Why did God require a blood sacrifice in His work of redemption?

ANSWER: The life of the flesh is in the blood, according to the Bible, as the Word says, "For the life of the flesh is in the blood: and I have given it to you upon the altar to make an atonement for your souls, for it is the blood that maketh an atonement for the soul.

"For it is the life of all flesh; the blood of it is for the life thereof: therefore I said unto the children of Israel, ye shall eat the blood of no manner of flesh: for the life of all flesh is the blood thereof: whosoever eateth it shall be cut off" (Leviticus 17:11&14).

When man disobeyed the direct command of God, he not only broke fellowship with his Father Creator, but also opened his life to corruption. The poison of sin entered his bloodstream and he began to die.

Through faith in God the Son, and the Great Redemptive Plan, our Lord provided His pure blood as a spiritual blood transfusion, and when our bodies are changed from corruption to incorruption, the poison of sin will be fully cleansed from our bloodstream and our blood will be as pure as the blood of our Savior.

Jesus alone paid the supreme price when He poured forth His life's blood, to cleanse us from all sin. His total sacrifice resulted in our total cleansing, as we receive by faith that which our heavenly Father offers us so freely.

QUESTION: Will our immortal, incorruptible bodies have blood, such as Adam had in his body before he sinned?

ANSWER: Yes, our immortal bodies will consist of flesh, blood and bones, like that of Adam and his wife, in the Garden of Eden, before they sinned. Otherwise, redemption would not be complete.

God has provided total redemption for His people, not merely a partial redemption. Let us praise Him for it.

The Promise and Provision of Redemption

Men in their ignorance and superstition have repeatedly rejected God and His will from their thinking, until they have bogged down in the deceitful quagmires of spiritual quicksand and the filthy pools of iniquity. In their foolishness they passed laws prohibiting the use of the Bible, the greatest book on earth, from their educational system, penalizing Christian students who were observed reading the Bibles, and boldly rejecting all references to the Bible and Christianity. Thank God, our nation is changing, slowly, but certainly.

The following article, concerning the Bible, is indeed inspiring, as selected by John Proffitt.

THE BIBLE: The Bible contains the mind of God, the state of man, the way of salvation, the doom of sinners and the happiness of believers. Its doctrines are holy, its precepts are binding, its histories are true, its decisions are immutable. Read it to be wise, believe it to be safe; practice it to be holy. It contains light to direct you, food to support you, comfort to cheer you.

It is the traveler's map, the pilgrim's staff, the pilot's compass, the soldier's sword, the Christian's charter. In it paradise is restored, heaven opened, hell disclosed. Christ is its grand subject, our good its design, God's glory its end. It should fill the memory, rule the heart and guide the feet. Read it slowly, frequently and prayerfully. It is a mine of wealth, a paradise of glory, and a river of pleasure. It is given you in life, will be open at judgement, and be remembered forever.

It involves the highest responsibility, rewards the greatest labor, and condemns all who trifle with its contents. It is a book of laws, to show the right from the wrong, a Book of wisdom that makes the foolish wise, a Book of truth, which detects all human errors;

A book of life, which shows how to avoid everlasting death. It is the most authentic and entertaining history ever published, an unequal narrative, a perfect body of divinity, a book of biography, a book of travels, the best Will ever executed, the best Deed ever written. It is the learned man's best companion, the schoolboy's best instructor, the ignorant man's dictionary and everybody's directory. But that which crowns all is the Author.

This manipulation of the Word, on the part of those who have failed to rely on the Holy Spirit, for correct interpretation and guidance, only succeeds in causing confusion, strife and division.

Just as God inspired and anointed Holy men of old to write the books of the Bible, many passages of which are prophetical and mysterious, so the Holy Spirit is well able to inspire and anoint holy men of our day to interpret the difficult passages of the Bible. All truly spiritually progressive believers must maintain open minds and hearts to receive continuing and increasing spiritual illumination from the Word.

Increasing revival comes through an increasing knowledge of the Word and will of God. God does not put new wine into old wine skins.

In this study we are endeavoring to bring to the attention of Bible-loving believers, certain promises of our heavenly Father, as they relate to His eternally increasing and expanding kingdom.

It is not difficult for human beings to develop doubts concerning the promises of God. Men and women of great faith have learned to believe the promises of God, not only in the intellect but also in the heart. The Psalmist said: "Thy Word have I hid in my heart, that I might not sin against you" (Psalm 119:11).

God has given us many precious promises, such as: "Blessed is the man who WALKETH not in the counsel of the ungodly, not

STANDETH in the way of sinners, not SITTETH in the seat of the scornful. But his delight is in the law of the Lord and in His law doth he meditate day and night. And he shall be like a tree planted by the rivers of water, that bringeth forth his fruit in his season; his leaf also shall not wither and whatsoever he doeth shall prosper" (Psalm 1:1–3).

Notice the contrast in the Psalm between the righteous and the ungodly.

God's promises invariably have certain conditions attached. Men desire the promises of God to be fulfilled in their lives, but they are unwilling to discipline themselves and put forth a determined effort to meet the conditions. God proves Himself, over and over again, to those who humbly and sincerely, in faith and with a positive confession, dare to claim the promises of God and appropriate them to themselves.

Consider the beautiful ninety-first Psalm. God's richest promises are fulfilled in the lives who have learned to: "Dwell in the secret place of the most High and dwell under the shadow of the Almighty." It is indeed inspiring to read and study the promises in this Psalm. Among other things the Lord promised, "With long life will I satisfy him, and show him My salvation" (Verse 16).

Our Lord has outlined the necessary steps that lead to an inner-circle relationship with Him, whereby His servants enjoy the fulfillment of His most precious promises. Why be satisfied with less than His best?

It is indeed a faith-building experience to study the many references pertaining to the promises of God. Time and attention devoted to such a study leads believers into a state of spiritual maturity. Those who have no time or personal interest in Bible study can never grow beyond the state of spiritual infancy.

The Bible tells us: "And I, brethren, could not speak unto you as unto spiritual, but as unto carnal, even as unto babes in Christ. I have fed you with milk, and not with meat: for hitherto you were not able to bear it, neither yet now are you able.

"For you are yet carnal: for whereas there is among you envying, and strife, and divisions, are you not carnal, and walk as men?" (1 Corinthians 3:1–3).

God wants His kids to grow and develop spiritually until we are able and willing to accept responsibility. We are not to choose our area of service, but rather to trust the Holy Spirit to direct us into the areas and type of ministry that God has chosen for us and called us to.

He also tells us: "For when for the time you ought to be teachers, you have need that one teach you again the first principles of the oracles of God; and are become such as have need of milk, and not strong meat" (Hebrews 5:12). When men are searching for gold, silver, precious gems, or other earthly riches, they deny themselves many comforts of life, digging and laboring for earthly treasure. And then many of them fail to reach their goals.

How much more should we Christians study, believe the promises of God, stand on His Word, discipline ourselves, and dig deeply into the Word of God for the precious gems of truth that bless, feed, and strengthen the soul.

Some years ago I read of two Americans, in particular, who sold their possessions in America and went to Australia to search for gold. The one man constructed his crude cabin and began his search, but he failed to discover gold.

In due time his funds were exhausted and he was on the verge of starvation. Too proud to request help or seek other employment, he became ill and died in poverty. After his death some farmers destroyed his cabin and while digging up the soil discovered gold where the cabin had been. The miner had lived and died above a rich vein of gold.

The other man discovered gold, had a large money belt filled with gold coins, and prepared to return to his homeland. He purchased a ticket on a ship, and out at sea, the ship encountered a severe storm, sprang a leak, and began to sink. There was an island within a reasonable distance, and the miner decided to swim to shore.

Passengers were drowning. A mother and her daughter were separated, and the mother was lost. The young girl clung to a piece of wreckage and cried for help. The miner was unable to save the girl and his heavy belt of gold also. He hesitated for only a moment, then unbuckled the belt and let the gold sink to the bottom of the sea. Taking the girl on his back, he swam to safety. He decided that her life was more valuable than the gold.

There are millions of lost souls out there, struggling in the stormy seas of life and hungry for God. Are we concerned about them, or are we self-satisfied, folding our arms and waiting for Jesus to come? He commanded His followers to: Occupy until His return. Are we doing it?

The best way to be ready for the rapture is to be occupied doing what He commanded us to do, when He said, "Go ye therefore, and teach all nations, baptizing them in the Name of the Father, and of the Son, and of the Holy Ghost" (Matt. 28:19).

Every spiritually progressive child of God is involved, one way or another, in helping to win lost souls and lead them to Jesus. If we cannot go personally, we can go by proxy, providing prayerful and financial support for those who are called of God to go.

The new and everlasting Covenant was sealed with the blood of Jesus: "In whom we have redemption, even the forgiveness of sins" (Colossians 1:14).

To accomplish the great work of redemption on earth, God chose to call us frail human beings into His service, that we may serve as His partners in this great ministry of world evangelism. The Bible says: "For after that in the wisdom of God the world by wisdom knew not God, it pleased God by the foolishness of preaching to save them that believe" (1 Corinthians 1:21).

He did not say, "By foolish preaching," but rather "By the foolishness of preaching."

However, we must acknowledge that God has a sense of humor. Billy Sunday said: "We know God has a sense of humor because He created the monkey, the parrot and some people." Jesus also has a sense of humor. On one occasion He referred to a certain class of religious people who were guilty of "straining at a gnat and swallowing a camel." In plain words they found the truth objectionable, but at the same time would swallow impossibilities. How about the evolutionist? Humor has its place in our Christian community, within certain limitations.

Like the uproar in a certain church where the pastor droned on and on in his dry and windy sermon. Finally little Tommy, who occupied space with his mother on a front pew, spoke loudly enough for all to hear: "Mother, are you sure this is the only way to heaven?" Needless to say, the pastor's discourse was suddenly terminated.

Years ago we had an evangelist friend who was conducting special services. One night he preached about Jonah. During the course of the message, he related an incident in which a pastor friend was preaching about Jonah. He waxed warm and eloquent and suddenly blurted out: "And Jonah swallowed the whale." Then our evangelist, desiring to emphasize a point, loudly stated, "And Jonah was in the whale of a belly."

Study: Focus Questions and Answers

QUESTION: If a person sins after his conversion, and continues in sin for a period of time, can he be forgiven and restored to fellowship with the Lord?

ANSWER: It would depend largely upon his attitude while living in a backslidden state. If his heart is still tender toward the Lord, and the Holy Spirit continues to bring condemnation upon him, for his sinful deeds, he can repent and receive God's forgiveness and cleansing.

QUESTION: Could you give me an example from the Bible in which a person or persons sinned, after having enjoyed fellowship with the Father, possessing the assurance of salvation, and then being restored?

ANSWER: Yes, I will give you two examples from the Bible, one in the Old Testament and one in the New.

Number one: King David committed heinous sins when he not only committed adultery, but had the woman's husband murdered. Later, when accused by Nathan the prophet, he repented of his sin and received forgiveness (2 Samuel 12:1–10). His prayer of repentance: "Have mercy upon me, O God, according to thy loving-kindness: according unto the multitude of thy tender mercies blot out my transgressions.

"Wash me thoroughly from my iniquity, and cleanse me from my sin. For I acknowledge my transgressions: and my sin is ever before me" (Psalm 51:1–3).

God forgave David and restored him to fellowship.

Number two: Peter boasted that he would never deny the Lord, yet in the time of crisis, he not only denied Him but added profane curses to his act of denial. But he later wept and repented of his sin: "And he denied it again. And a little after, they that stood by said again to Peter, Surely thou art one of them: for thou art a Galilean, and thy speech agreeth thereto. But he began to curse and to swear, saying, I know not this man of whom ye speak" (Mark 14:70,71). He remembered the Lord's words and wept (verse 72).

The Rewards and Responsibilities of Redemption

God has promised to reward His servants according to our works. The Word tells us: "For other foundation can no man lay than that is laid, which is Jesus Christ. Now if any man build upon this foundation gold, silver, precious stones, wood, hay, stubble; Every man's work shall be made manifest: for the day shall declare it, because it shall be revealed by fire; and the fire shall try every man's work of what sort it is.

"If any man's work abide which he has built thereupon, he shall receive a reward. If any man's work shall be burned, he shall suffer loss: but he himself shall be saved; yet so as by fire" (1 Cor. 3:11–15).

We choose whether to use indestructible materials compared to gold, silver, and precious stones, or destructible materials compared to wood, hay, and stubble. When God accomplishes His work through our lives, He uses His materials, the very divine attributes of Himself. When men use their own materials such as human ambitions, worldly enthusiasm, and selfish desires, relying on their human intellect, there will be no reward.

God judges us according to our willingness to be prayerfully led by His Holy Spirit, totally surrendered to His will, and living the life by His grace, that brings glory to Him alone. You may have heard of the conversation between two pastors. One said "I preached a hell and brimstone sermon to my congregation last Sunday." The other one said, "Did you preach it in love?"

When God judges us human beings, He judges the heart and

takes into consideration the motives, the environment, the person's heredity and other important factors.

Positions of honor and responsibility in this life are no guarantee of increasing honor in the future life. God requires faithfulness in little things as well as greater. His Holy Spirit directs in accomplishing good works.

As many are reluctant to accept responsibility in the natural, so it is in the spiritual. There is a tendency on the part of some to extend their childish attitudes, conduct, and lack of responsibility on through life. Those who refrain from accepting responsibility both in the natural realm as well as the spiritual, are never able to achieve a feeling of absolute security in life.

We have observed down through the years when children are deprived of proper discipline and direction they grow to adulthood with the attitude that anything will do. God's kids are prone to feel that it is not their responsibility to assist in sharing the burdens of paying God's tithe, giving of their offerings, or accepting responsible positions in the church, such as teaching, playing instruments, singing, or developing their God-given ability to His honor and glory.

I very well remember when I was about five years of age, or less, that my father made me responsible to see that the woodbox was filled each evening. One evening I forgot and Dad taught me a lesson that blessed me throughout my life. He had no wood to start the fire in the kitchen range the following morning, so he called me from a sound sleep, about 5:00 A.M. to get out of bed and go out and bring in the wood. I remembered every evening after that.

When we are properly disciplined early in life, always in love, we learn to discipline ourselves. Whether we eat, or drink, or whatever we do, we desire to do all to the glory of God. There will invariably be mistakes along this journey of life, but generally we learn more through our failures than we do through our successes. The important thing is to maintain open minds so that we are able to learn valuable lessons that sustain us in the years to come. Increasing knowledge is never imparted to those who maintain closed minds and hearts. The Holy Spirit does not force spiritual illumination upon us. We must hunger and thirst after knowledge and the righteousness of God.

God's rewards will not only consist of salvation from sin and the positive assurance of our participation in His glorious, eternal kingdom, but also positions of honor and responsibility in His kingdom, for His mature servants who are spiritually and otherwise qualified, by His grace. There will be no curse on the New Earth. That includes the curse God placed upon woman, man, and the earth itself.

When God created man, male and female, He commanded them to multiply in the Garden of Eden. Obviously, the rate of reproduction, prior to the Fall, was much less than after the Fall, otherwise, how could God have increased woman's pain and conceptions relating to childbirth?

Yes, the Bible teaches that babies will be born in the future life, but when the curse is lifted from redeemed, immortal women, the rate of reproduction will be greatly decreased, and there will be very little pain in connection with childbirth. We may not understand all changes related to the future life, but we believe what the Bible teaches.

God knew from the beginning the number of sons and daughters He would have when the New Earth is prepared for habitation. He therefore increased woman's conceptions to make allowance for multiplied millions who will be lost, because of rejecting Christ Jesus as Redeemer. When we arrive on the New Earth, God will have the exact number of redeemed souls He would have had if man had never sinned. God cannot be defeated.

Greater knowledge concerning the future life provides an added incentive and inducement for receiving Christ Jesus as Savior and living a victorious life. We have received much information concerning what we are saved from, but God also has made provision for us to possess some knowledge concerning what we are saved for and to.

The Holy Spirit is waiting and ready to guide hungry, searching souls into a deepening relationship with our Lord, through increasing knowledge of the Word and will of God.

The question has been asked, by those who love God and His Word: "Why did God create billions of galaxies?" We all must agree that He has a purpose in all that He does. Isaiah wrote the following words by divine inspiration: "For unto us a child is born, unto us a Son is given: and the government shall be upon His shoulder: and His Name shall be called Wonderful, Counselor, the mighty God, The everlasting Father, the Prince of Peace.

Of the *INCREASE OF HIS GOVERNMENT AND PEACE, THERE SHALL BE NO END,* upon the throne of David, and upon his kingdom, to order it, and to establish it with judgement and with justice from henceforth even forever. The zeal of the Lord of hosts will perform this" (Isaiah 9:6,7).

Astronomers who have searched the heavens, with their powerful telescopes, tell us there are billions of galaxies in outer space. Each time they manufacture a more powerful telescope, they discover more galaxies. Our galaxy has some 240 million solar systems and each solar system has an average of eight to ten planets. Could it be that God is preparing these multiplied billions of solar systems for an increasing population on into the never-ending future eternity? He does not require an increasing government unless He plans for an increasing population.

THE BIBLE TEACHES THAT A STATE OF REPRODUCTION WILL EXIST AMONG THE REDEEMED, IMMORTAL SAINTS OF GOD, ON AND ON INTO THAT ENDLESS, ETERNAL FUTURE. NOTICE CAREFULLY AND PRAYERFULLY THE FOLLOWING SCRIPTURAL REFERENCE:

Lo, children are an heritage of the Lord: and the fruit of the womb is His reward (Psalm 127:3).

Thy wife shall be a fruitful vine by the sides of your house: your children like olive plants round about your table. Behold, that thus shall the man be blessed that feareth the Lord (Psalm 128:3,4).

If Adam and his wife had not sinned, they would have continued reproducing eternally.

Dr. J.E. Seiss, in his book, *The Apocalypse* (chapter 48 and page 483), states as follows: "I therefore hold it to be a necessary and integral part of the Scriptural doctrine of human redemption, that our race, as a self-multiplying order of beings, will never cease either to exist or to possess the earth."

His teachings are both scriptural and practical, and they are definitely the best material I have ever studied concerning God's plan of redemption, apart from the Bible.

Every good law that God instituted from the beginning is eternal. All laws that were instituted after man fell were designed to serve only a temporary purpose, for this life alone. The Bible tells us that generations are to succeed one another eternally. Notice what the Lord tells us:

Your kingdom is an *EVERLASTING* kingdom, and your dominion throughout *ALL GENERATIONS* (Psalm 145:13).

The Lord shall reign *FOREVER,* even your God, unto all *GENERATIONS.* Praise ye the Lord (Psalm 146:10).

Prophecies pertaining to the future life extend far beyond the Millennial reign and will reach total fulfillment on the New Earth, and on into our Lord's increasing kingdom throughout the New Heavens also. Prayerfully consider the following prophecies:

The wolf shall dwell with the lamb, and the leopard shall lie down with the kid; and the calf and the young lion and the fatling together; and a *LITTLE CHILD* shall lead them. And the cow and the

34

bear shall feed; their young ones shall lie down together: and the lion shall eat straw like the ox. And the *SUCKING CHILD* shall play on the hole of the asp (cobra), and the *WEANED CHILD* shall put his hand on the cockatrice's (viper's) den. They shall not hurt nor destroy in all my holy mountain: for the earth shall be full of the knowledge of the Lord, as the waters cover the sea (Isa.11:6–9).

This will be a reality when the sons of God have received their inheritance (Romans 8:16–23).

Sin and death will continue into the Millennial reign, as the mortal segment of earth's population will continue to multiply on earth through the thousand-year period also. These prophecies, therefore, will not be totally fulfilled until the immortal population will be established on the New Earth. At which time, Roman 8:19,20 will be fulfilled, which reads: "For the earnest expectation of the creature (creation) waiteth for the manifestation of the sons of God. Because the creature itself also shall be delivered from the bondage of corruption into the glorious liberty of the sons of God."

Isaiah also prophesied of events that are to transpire on the New Earth. Read the following references prayerfully:

As for me, this is my covenant with them, saith the Lord; My Spirit that is upon you, and my words which I have put in your mouth, shall not depart out of your mouth, nor out of the mouth of your descendants, nor out of the mouth of your descendant's descendants, saith the Lord, from henceforth and forever (Isaiah 59:21, KJV, Modern English).

The sun shall no longer be your light by day; neither for brightness shall the moon give light unto you, but the Lord shall be unto you an everlasting light, and your God your glory. Your sun shall no more go down; neither shall the moon withdraw itself: for the Lord shall be your everlasting light, and the days of your mourning shall be ended.

Your people also shall be all righteous: they shall inherit the land forever, the branch of my planting, the work of my hands, that I may be glorified.

A little one shall become a THOUSAND, and a small one a STRONG NATION: I the Lord will hasten it in his time (Isaiah 60:19–22, KJV).

These prophecies from the Book of Isaiah will be fulfilled on the New Earth, as indicated in Revelation 21:23,24.

Ezekiel the prophet was inspired to write prophecy as it relates to the future life. Notice the following passage:

And David My servant shall be king over them; and they shall have one shepherd: they shall also walk in my judgements, and observe My statutes, and do them.

And they shall dwell in the land that I have given to Jacob My servant, wherein your fathers have dwelt; and they shall dwell therein, even they, and their children, and their children's children forever; and My servant David shall be their Prince forever.

Moreover I will make a covenant of peace with them: it shall be an everlasting covenant with them; and I will place them, and multiply them, and I will set My sanctuary in the midst of them for evermore (Ezekiel 37:24–26).

Some well-meaning Bible teachers have concluded that the prophet was referring to our Lord Jesus Christ, rather than King David himself. Jesus is referred to as the "Son of David," but never called "David." Notice Matthew 1:1, for example: "The book of genealogy of Jesus Christ, the Son of David, the Son of Abraham."

In studying the Scriptures, some are prone to equate certain Bible passages to the future life, when they pertain only to this present life. Certain temporary laws have been instituted on earth, since the Fall of man, that apply only to this life. They will all be abolished when the redeemed children of God are ushered out into the future life, in God's perfect kingdom. Permanent laws, which God instituted in the past eternity, will again function, according to His plan in the future eternity, such as all spiritual laws, laws of nature, laws in the heavenlies, and throughout His vast, endless universal system.

When Jesus spoke to the unbelieving Sadducees, concerning the woman who had seven husbands, He was referring to the legality of marriage, in its many forms. All such laws were to serve in this life only.

The law of the LEVIRATE allowed polygamy in Israel during the administration of the Mosaic Law. If a man died leaving no children, a brother or close relative was obligated to marry the widow. The unbelieving Sadducees did not believe in a physical resurrection when they questioned Jesus concerning the woman who had seven husbands, one at a time. Their question was: "Therefore, in the resurrection, whose wife will she be?"

Jesus never explained the mysteries of the eternal kingdom of God to unbelievers. He did not say there would be no mating among HIS redeemed people in the future life. He simply said, "Ye do err, not knowing the scriptures or the power of God. For in the resurrection they neither marry, nor are given in marriage, but are as the angels of God in heaven" (Matthew 22:29,30).

In simple words: God will join couples together by His Holy Spirit, as He did in the Garden of Eden. Man-made ceremonies will be abolished. Jesus said, "What therefore God hath joined together, let not man put asunder" (Mark 10:9).

Laws of sin and death will not exist in the future life, but all of the redeemed will be subject to eternal laws: "For the law of the Spirit of life in Christ Jesus has made me free from the law of sin and death" (Romans 8:2).

Couples whom God has joined together in this life will undoubtedly be together eternally. As generations follow generations, the Holy Spirit will unite couples according to the will of God. If man is not to put couples asunder, certainly God Himself will not do so.

Old covenants, instituted after man fell, will be obsolete and

God's immortal, redeemed saints will live under the New Covenant laws, sealed by the precious blood of Jesus Christ Himself. Is this too impossible to believe? The old temporary laws were to function until Christ came to bring in the New Covenant. Read Galatians 3:19.

When we enter into a personal relationship with Christ Jesus, through faith in God, because of His love, mercy, and grace, our sins are forgiven and we begin the walk with Him who leads us ever onward and upward. We have that positive assurance that: "He has delivered us from the power of darkness and conveyed us into the kingdom of the Son of His love, in whom we have redemption through His blood, the forgiveness of sins" (Col. 1:13,14, NKJV).

God's purpose is to lift every curse from men, women, and the earth itself. He will accomplish a total work of redemption and restoration. This will be fulfilled when the redeemed are established on the New Earth. Notice what He tells us: "And there shall be no more curse, but the throne of God and the Lamb shall be in it, and His servants shall serve Him" (Revelation 22:3).

Some question the advisability of teaching prophetical passages relating to the future life. We are living in the end of this age. The world is passing through a transitional period in preparation for the Millennial reign. Knowledge in all areas of human thinking is increasing, and God is leading His servants into greater spiritual understanding. Jesus said: "It is written, that man shall not live by bread alone, but by every Word of God" (Luke 4:4).

God's original desire was for man to live eternally in his righteousness, with an immortal body consisting of flesh, blood and bones. Had man done so, he would have continued reproducing gradually, forever. If we do not believe that, we would have to agree that children are from the devil. Every good thing God created is eternal.

Because of man's sin, God's eternal plan was temporarily

disrupted, but only temporarily. His work of total redemption is in the process of being fulfilled, so that every good thing he gave man in the beginning will be restored permanently, to His redeemed immortal children.

Why not plan now to enjoy God's best, eternally?

When man sinned in the Garden of Eden, God promised a Redeemer. "So the Lord said to the serpent: because you have done this, You are cursed more than all cattle, And more than every beast of the field; On your belly you shall go, and you shall eat dust All the days of your life.

"And I will put enmity Between you and the woman, and between your seed and her Seed; He shall bruise your head, And you shall bruise His heel" (Gen. 3:14,15; NKJV).

In the year of 1950, while I was engaged in a deliverance revival, God spoke to me one night in a vision. It seemed that I was alone in a large auditorium when suddenly a door opened in the floor and a huge serpent came toward me. I was seeking a way of escape when the Lord spoke to me and said: "You have challenged the devil, now face him." I faced him in the Name of the Lord and we battled in the area. Finally, I had my left hand behind his head, with my left knee behind it, and was beating him on the head with a weapon. It was the Word of God. Each time I struck a blow, he screamed hideously. Then I noticed that his head was bruised and bleeding and I said, "Satan, I did not inflict these wounds on your head, but my master did, and in His name I am also your conqueror." At that moment he withdrew and retreated into the pit.

In this life we are called upon to face numerous challenges, but rest assured, when we face them in the Name of the Lord, and in His strength, we are victorious.

As the people of God, we are engaged in a constant spiritual conflict, but without the battle, there can be no victory. Each time we engage in a spiritual battle, and win a victory, we move to a higher spiritual level. If we are fearful and unbelieving, refusing to accept the challenge, there will be no victory and we continue to move in religious circles in the state of mediocrity.

Our Lord desires to lead us from glory to glory.

Study: Focus—Questions and Answers

QUESTION: Could you give me two specific Bible references concerning God's promise of redemption?

ANSWER: Yes, certainly. There are many more than two, but I will give you two. "We have redemption through His blood, the forgiveness of sins, according to the riches of His grace" (Ephesians 1:7).

"Neither by the blood of goats and calves, but by His own blood He entered in once into the Holy Place, having obtained eternal redemption for us" (Hebrews 9:12).

QUESTION: How can a person know they have not crossed the deadline, as it were, and can no longer be saved?

ANSWER: If a person has sinned away their day of grace, and the Holy Spirit no longer deals with their conscience, or brings them under condemnation, their heart will be hardened, a spirit of unbelief will possess them, and they will have no desire to receive Christ as Savior and Lord.

QUESTION: Are you telling us then that deathbed repentances are not acceptable in the sight of the Lord?

ANSWER: No, it depends on whether or not the Holy Spirit is drawing a person to Himself. The Bible says: "No man can come to Me, except the Father which has sent Me draw him: and I raise him up at the last day" (John 6:44).

People who gamble with their never-dying soul are running a great risk of spending the future eternity in the lake of fire.

QUESTION: What responsibilities must I accept, if I am to be rewarded at the judgement of rewards?

ANSWER: May I first of all ask you a question? Do you desire a great reward or only the assurance of escaping hell and living in God's eternal kingdom?

If you sincerely desire God's best, you must give Him your best, by submitting sincerely to His Word and will, loving the Word, living in the Word, and demonstrating faith in the Word. Otherwise, as a spiritual baby, you need not expect any special reward.

Appendix A

A Comparison: Contrast of Creation in Genesis and the Re-creation in Revelation

GENESIS	REVELATION
creation (man, animals, habitat)	re-creation
satan and sin enter	sin and satan exit
first Adam's choice brings judgement and death	second Adam (Jesus Christ) brings life and redemption
PARADISE LOST	PARADISE REGAINED
satan's reign begins	satan's reign ends
the Tree of Life is canceled	the Tree of Life is reinstated
the eternal fellowship of purity between Creator and His creation is broken	the eternal fellowship of purity between Creator and His creation is healed by the blood of the Lamb, Jesus Christ

Note: In this study we have used scriptural references from the KJV and the NKJV only. We appreciate the NKJV because of the modern English, but we believe that the regular KJV is the most authentic translation.

Appendix B

Supplementary Questions and Answers

QUESTION: If God's plan for the future ages includes His eternal laws of productivity, will immortal children of God have the same mates they have in this present life?

ANSWER: If couples are perfectly mated in this life, and desire to be together as husband and wife eternally, there is no reason why it should be otherwise.

It is also a fact that in many marriages the couples are mismated and they never seem to be able to fully adjust to one another so as to enjoy mutual love, harmony, and face the problems of life with united minds and hearts.

One man expressed his doubts by saying, "I would not want to be married to the same old woman forever." Many of the ladies feel that way about their husbands also. God will not have mismatched couples in His eternal economy. He does all things perfect.

QUESTION: How will we know whether or not we have the mate God has chosen for us?

ANSWER: God's people, in this present life, are living on different spiritual frequencies. It is difficult for those in God's kindergarten to communicate normally with those in His university. The lack of normal communication in the marriage relationship results in disruptions and quite frequently divorce, even among Christian couples.

We conclude therefore, through logic and association, that couples will be mated and united in the future life under the direction of the Holy Spirit of God, who does all things well. God is a miracle-working God and well able to establish relationships that will be eternal, fulfilling, rewarding and productive.

QUESTION: Then you are telling us that we may not have the same mate in the future life that we have in this life?

ANSWER: Yes, marriages in this life are intended to be regulated by laws. The Bible tells us that when one person dies, the living widow or widower is free to remarry. "Know ye not, brethren, (for I speak to them that know the law) how that the law hath dominion over a man as long as he liveth? For the woman which hath an husband is bound by the law to her husband so long as he liveth; but if the husband be dead, she is loosed from the law of her husband" (Rom. 7:1,2).

These temporary laws will all be abolished. God will have a new set of laws in the future life, eternal laws, and all of His redeemed saints will be subject to them.

Jesus said: "But from the beginning of the creation God made them male and female" (Mark 10:6). Undoubtedly this includes all forms of life God created in the very beginning, long before man was created.

QUESTION: Then those who have never found a mate in this life may look forward to being perfectly mated in the future life, if they so desire?

ANSWER: Yes, if we believe that God does all things well, and that He knows the end from the beginning, all of His people who so desire may be perfectly mated in the future life, on the same spiritual frequency, as the Holy Spirit directs. This also applies to those whose wives or husbands are lost. God will provide new mates.

But remember, the rate of reproduction will be greatly diminished, because the curse upon the redeemed women will be lifted. Pain in childbirth will be greatly decreased also. What would heaven be without little children?

QUESTION: Will this perfect relationship exist upon earth during the Millennial Reign?

ANSWER: The Bible prophecies indicate that many wonderful improvements will be made on earth, when our Lord establishes His literal kingdom on earth, but there will continue to be laws governing the mortal element of earth's population until the end of the Millennial reign. All things will be different when we are established on the New Earth. Now is the time for us to be prepared for better things.

QUESTION: Does the Bible make a distinction between the so-called natural people and the immortal children of God?

ANSWER: Not to my knowledge. God created man, male and female, according to the natural laws in His divine pattern of Creation. He created them in His own likeness and image, so man was created in the likeness of God Himself. Had he created them with fewer attributes, they would have been subnormal. Had He created them with greater attributes, they would have been abnormal. He created them as normal, natural people, with immortal, incorruptible bodies, and they shared His glory.

But, when they sinned, they lost their immortality and their bodies became corruptible. In their mortal state, they became subnormal. They deteriorated in spirit, soul, and body. God in His love, grace, and mercy has provided the great redemptive plan, so that through the process of redemption, man is being restored to his former normal state, and as a natural, normal being will possess everything God gave him in the beginning, and be everything that God intended for him to be.

This is all to be fulfilled when redeemed, immortal men, women, and children experience the miraculous change, from mortality to immortality, as He promised, and as the Bible states: "Behold, I show you a mystery; We shall not all sleep, (die) but we shall *ALL* be changed" (1 Cor.15:51).

The change is from mortality to immortality, as the following verses tell us. All redeemed children of God must die, according to Hebrews 9:27, and be resurrected in their immortal state, or be changed to immortality as at the moment of their translation, referred to as the rapture. God's redeemed, immortal saints will all be one in Christ and continue to function eternally according to God's original plan, as revealed in the Garden of Eden.

RESOURCE MATERIALS AND ORDER FORMS

Reesor, J.B. *God's Guide to Man's Future.*
409 31st Avenue South
Nashville, TN 37212
Seiss, J.E. *The Apocalypse.*
Sunderland, L.D. *Darwin's Enigma.* Master Book Publishers, Santee, Calif.
Goodyear, J.H.111. *Pure Words: Which English Bible Translation Is Most Accurate?* Plank Press, Grantham, PA.
Goodyear, J.H.111. *The Principle of Promise-Condition-Choice.* Plank Press, Grantham, PA.

These resources may be ordered from the publishers. (NOTE: Any contribution you may feel led to send to the Nashvile address will be greatly appreciated, as many of the books will be donated to workers on the mission field who cannot afford to pay for them. Thank you.)

ORDER FORM

Author and Title

( ) Reesor, J.B. *God's Guide to Man's Future*
( ) Seiss, J.E. *The Apocalypse*
( ) Sunderland, L.D. *Darwin's Enigma*
( ) Goodyear, J.H.111. *Pure Words . . .*
( ) Goodyear, J.H.111. *Principle of Promise-Condition-Choice.*
( ) Reesor and Goodyear. *God's Grand Redemptive Design*

Heaven's
Most Glorious
Celebration

Foreword

Dr. Reesor and I became acquainted in 1980 when he was serving as Director of the School of Ministry at Bethany Tabernacle in Camp Hill, Pennsylvania. After a Wednesday night service, while we were visiting, he invited me to accompany him on a missionary trip to the Philippines, which began a ministry of missionary work for us.

Through our personal acquaintance and friendship, I developed great respect for Rev. Reesor's ability to minister in extreme conditions. We traveled together and I have seen him minister to great numbers of people and also in small churches with bamboo walls, a thatch roof, and dirt floors. His message is always clear and to the point.

Writing this "FOREWORD" is a great privilege for me. The message of "HEAVEN'S MOST GLORIOUS CELEBRATION," with special rewards shared with God's faithful servants, will challenge us to be all that God has called us to be, and to accomplish those things for us to accomplish in our lifetime. It is my personal opinion that the Bible truth contained within these pages will have a real life-changing influence for you and all that will travel through these pages.

Milton "Leo" Nehrt, B.A.
Executive Pilot-Retired
Missionary-at-Large

Introduction

To undertake the task of preparing a biblical study of this particular subject requires, not only concentrated, prayerful study of all related Scriptural references, plus total reliance upon the illuminating guidance of the Holy Spirit, but also a charitable attitude toward all conclusions on the part of capable Bible teachers.

The author has arrived at certain personal convictions and conclusions as a result of many years of prayerful study. In his years of teaching on the subject, he has received ample evidence from truth-seeking individuals that this teaching has proven to serve as an added inducement toward a deepening spiritual experience and a more dedicated lifestyle in soul-winning effort.

In the early years of the latter-rain outpouring of the Holy Spirit, certain Bible teachers made a distinction between the Bride of Christ and the major Body of Christ, which is the Church. In more recent years, Spirit-filled men are teaching the existence of a mature body of believers within the Christian community.

It is the desire of the author to permit the Scriptures to speak for themselves, as the Holy Spirit provides the necessary inspiration and guidance. Jesus said: "But the Comforter, which is the Holy Ghost, whom the Father will send in My Name, He shall teach you all things, and bring all things to your remembrance, whatsoever I have said unto you" (John 14:26).

Major Celebrations in Heaven

In all probability there have been numerous celebrations in heaven during the past eternal ages, but in this study we wish to introduce a limited number that are implied in the biblical record.

In one of the Lord's conversations with Job, the Lord said, "Where were you when I laid the foundations of the earth? Tell Me, if you have understanding. Who determined its measurements? Surely you know! Or who stretched the line upon it? To what were its foundations fastened? Or who laid its cornerstone, When the morning stars sang together, And all the sons of God shouted for Joy?" (Job 38:4–7).

Our English word "sons" as used in verse 7, is translated from the Hebrew word "BEN," pronounced "bane," meaning "one born" and our English word "daughters" is translated from the same Hebrew word. We may safely conclude that the phrase "sons of God" also includes daughters of God, or to express it concisely, both male and female. Think of the great celebration the angelic sons and daughters of God enjoyed when the Lord created planet Earth, and appointed Lucifer, one of the leading angels, as ruler over his third of the angels at that time.

Had Lucifer and his angels been satisfied to remain in fellowship and harmony with the triune Godhead and continued in a spirit of submission to the will of God, peace and a state of divine tranquility would have continued. Because of a spirit of pride, which possessed Lucifer, and an ambitious determination to enlarge his kingdom, he led his angels into heaven in open defiance and warfare. The passage in Ezekiel 28:13–15, undoubtedly applies to Lucifer, rather than to the king of Tyre. Notice what the Bible tells us:

"You were in Eden, the garden of God; Every precious stone was your covering: . . . The workmanship of your timbrels and pipes was prepared for you on the day you were created.

"You were the anointed cherub who covers; I established you; You were on the holy mountain of God; You walked back and forth in the midst of fiery stones, you were perfect in your ways from the day you were created, Till iniquity was found in you" (NKJV).

The above descriptive passage implies that the anointed cherub, who was presumably none other than Lucifer himself, became proud and arrogant in his kingly position over the angelic nations on planet Earth, originally called "EDEN," so he decided to engage in warfare against God's loyal angels in a determined effort to extend his own kingdom. This effort on his part, as described in Isaiah 14:12–15 was, however, an abortive move and resulted in his absolute defeat.

Again, we may readily imagine that there was a victorious celebration in heaven, among God's loyal angelic subjects, when Lucifer and his angels were cast out and he became Satan, the adversary, commonly referred to as the devil. Yes, there is indeed a personal devil, whether some people believe it or not. To doubt the existence of the devil certainly does not necessitate his departure into a state of oblivion. As prince and power of the air, and the god of this world, satan is determined to destroy as many ungodly, impenitent, gullible souls as possible. Our only place of refuge from his evil power and influence is in Christ Jesus our Lord. He is our hiding place.

Then we are able to understand another celebration in heaven when the Triune Godhead accomplished the work of re-creation, when the planet Eden was restored to its original beauty, with plant life, animals, birds, fish, and then man to have dominion over it all. Our beneficent Heavenly Father no doubt announced to His angelic population that His purpose in creating man was to fulfill His original plan for an increasing population and fellowship.

The reality of life in the heavenly realm far exceeds our most vivid imagination. We are so prone to equate life in heaven with familiar conditions on earth, and it is a fact that when we arrive in heaven we will certainly recognize many heavenly benefits that will remind us of the best of life here on earth, but the glory and reality will be much greater. The very word "HEAVEN" implies a place of glory, beauty, joy, happiness, and activity.

Please imagine with me the sorrow and apprehension that undoubtedly prevailed in heaven when Jesus, God the Son, volunteered to descend to earth and be born of the virgin Mary, that He may become 100 percent man, as well as 100 percent God, and pay the supreme price for our redemption, when He went to Calvary and died on a cruel cross in our place.

But then, imagine also what a joyful celebration it was when our Savior, the blessed Son of God, accomplished the work of redemption, declaring, "IT IS FINISHED" and then ascended to heaven to take His rightful place at the right hand of the Father.

It is not difficult to believe that numerous other major celebrations have transpired in heaven, since the day of man's creation, and we are confident there will be others in the future. Consider the time of the rapture of the living saints of God and the resurrection of the righteous, prior to the beginning of the seventieth week of Daniel, seven years of time in which God will devote much attention to the spiritual restoration of Israel. When multitudes of the redeemed are suddenly caught up to meet the Lord in the air, and taken on into heaven for the great judgment of rewards, meeting with loved ones and friends who have gone on before, what a grand reunion it will be. Certainly, there will be a major celebration in heaven.

But, the Scriptures give us a beautiful word picture of the greatest celebration of all. Think about it.

Christ Our Heavenly Bridegroom

As our heavenly Bridegroom, He is certainly no ordinary person. He is indeed 100 percent man and 100 percent God. As God he created all things and was coexistent with the Father from the very beginning, somewhere in the past eternity. As the Word says, "In the beginning was the Word, and the Word was with God, and the Word was God. He was in the beginning with God. All things were made by Him, and without Him was not anything made that was made. In Him was life, and the life was the light of men" (John 1:1–4).

Jesus referred to Himself as the Bridegroom: the disciples of John and of the Pharisees were fasting. Then they came and said to Him, "Why do the disciples of John and the Pharisees fast, but your disciples do not fast?" And Jesus said to them, "Can the friends of the bridegroom fast while the bridegroom is yet with them? As long as they have the bridegroom with them they cannot fast. But the days will come when the bridegroom will be taken away from them, and then shall they fast in those days" (Mark 2:18–20, NKJV).

As our heavenly Bridegroom, He is also our Savior, our Lord, and our friend, and He desires that we respond to His friendship by endeavoring to become worthy of His friendship, as the Bible says, "A man that hath friends must show himself friendly: and there is a friend that sticketh closer than a brother" (Proverbs 18:24).

Jesus also said, "This is my commandment, that you love one another as I have loved you. Greater love has no man than this, than to lay down one's life for his friends. You are My friends, if you do whatever I command you. No longer do I call you servants, for a servant does not know what his master is doing; but I have called you friends, for all things that I heard from My Father I have made known unto you" (John 15:12–15).

When we love Him as we ought to, we will pray for strength and guidance to obey Him as we ought to. In so doing we enjoy His approval and blessing.

John the Baptist also referred to Jesus as the bridegroom, when he said, "He who has the bride is the bridegroom; but the friend of the bridegroom, who stands and hears him, rejoices greatly because of the bridegroom's voice. Therefore this joy of mine is fulfilled" (John 3:29).

Those who are married to Christ, in this present life, are to bear fruit to God, as the Bible says: "Therefore, my brethren, you also have become dead to the law through the body of Christ, that you may be married to another—to Him who was raised from the dead, that we should bear fruit to God" (Rom. 7:4).

Jesus warns His followers concerning the tragedy that will befall them if they fail to bear fruit. Notice what He tells us: "I am the vine, you are the branches. He who abides in Me, and I in him, bears much fruit; for without Me you can do nothing. If anyone does not abide in Me, he is cast out as a branch and is withered; and they gather them and throw them into the fire, and they are burned" (John 15:5,6).

Our marriage to Christ does not involve a civil ceremony, performed by man, but is a spiritual union accomplished by the Holy Spirit. When this spiritual union leads to an intimate relationship with Christ, believers become fruitful. The productive child of God is a soul-winning Christian, one way or another, through a personal ministry, such as preaching, teaching, singing, praying, witnessing, giving, and in other ways.

As God and man, Jesus came to manifest the love of God and demonstrate the power of God. As the only Way, the only Truth, and the only source of divine life, He came to reveal God to a fallen, debased, and disgraced human race and lead believers to a life of victory and accomplishment. He freely gave Himself, as a total sacrifice, to redeem us from satan's slave market and lead us into eternal light.

During our Lord's ministry on earth, He preached much concerning the kingdom of heaven, and in so doing set the example for His disciples. The Bible tells us: "And Jesus went about all Galilee, teaching in their synagogues, preaching the Gospel of the kingdom, and healing all kinds of sickness and all kinds of disease among the people" (Matt. 4:23).

Wherever He went the multitudes flocked out to hear Him and be blessed by His ministry. When truth is preached in love and sincerity, under the anointing and direction of the Holy Spirit, people will listen, learn, and grow spiritually. There are those, whom Jesus referred to, who feel that "they have arrived," and in their tendency toward compromise, and self-aggrandizement, they strive to promote themselves. Jesus refers to them as trees. He said, "Every tree that does not bear good fruit is cut down and thrown into the fire. Therefore by their fruits you will know them. Not everyone who says to Me, Lord, Lord, shall enter into the kingdom of heaven, but he who does the will of My Father in heaven.

"Many will say to Me in that day, Lord, Lord, have we not prophesied in your Name, cast out devils in your Name, and done wonders in Your Name? And then I will declare to them, I never knew you; depart from Me, you who practice lawlessness!" (Matt. 7:19–23).

Self-reliance in the accomplishment of the ministry our Lord has called us to can only result in personal loss. Those who lean heavily upon the Lord, trusting in the power and guidance of the Holy Spirit, preaching and teaching the blessed Word of God under His anointing and direction, will enjoy a rich harvest of souls.

Jesus, our heavenly Bridegroom, has a threefold ministry, as

Prophet, Priest, and King. Moses prophesied concerning our Lord's ministry as a Prophet (Deut. 18:15).

The prophecy of Moses was fulfilled in the life of Jesus, as we read: "For Moses truly said unto the fathers, A prophet shall the Lord your God raise up unto you of your brethren, like unto me; Him shall ye hear in all things whatsoever He shall say unto you. And it shall come to pass, that every soul, which will not hear that prophet, shall be destroyed from among the people" (Acts 3:22,23).

The people also recognized Jesus as a prophet because of what He said and did. The Bible says: "Then those men, when they had seen the miracle that Jesus did, said, This is of a truth that prophet that should come into the world" (John 6:14).

Jesus also referred to Himself as a prophet when He said, "A prophet is not without honor, save in his own country and in his own house" (Matt. 13:57). God's prophets, when used of the Lord, speak God's words to men and our Lord and Savior was and is the greatest of them all. In our day there are spiritually mature men who occupy the office of a prophet, as part of the fivefold ministry gifts, and their prophecies will always correspond with the Bible.

There is also the gift of prophecy, as one of the gifts of the Spirit, and when it is operating God's mature sons will judge (1 Cor. 14:29–32).

Not only is our heavenly bridegroom a prophet, but He is also our great High Priest, according to the Bible: "Seeing then that we have a great High Priest, who has passed through the heavens, Jesus the Son of God, let us hold fast our confession. For we do not have an High Priest who cannot sympathize with our weaknesses, but was in all points tempted as we are, yet without sin. Let us therefore come boldly to the throne of grace, that we may obtain mercy and find grace to help in time of need" (Hebrews 4:14–16).

Jesus, our great High Priest and heavenly Bridegroom, is seated at the side of our heavenly Father, interceding for us, that we may continue faithful.

God has called many of His faithful children to a ministry of intercessory prayer and the results have been incredible. Jesus, in His High Priestly office, accomplishes an eternal work of restoration in the yielded lives of His dedicated servants.

Our heavenly Bridegroom is not only the greatest of all prophets and high priests, but also the King of kings and Lord of lords. Therefore, as Prophet, Priest, and King He will be the supreme ruler over all other appointed rulers and officials throughout our Father's eternal kingdom. He will make the appointments according to the level of spiritual qualifications that His servants have attained in this present life.

Because of His love, His servants are becoming what He intends for them to be. The Word says, "And from Jesus Christ, the faithful witness, the firstborn from the dead, and the ruler over the kings of the earth. To Him who loved us and washed us from our sins in His own blood, and has made us kings and priests to His God and father, to Him be glory and dominion forever and ever. Amen" (Rev. 1:5,6).

To respond properly to His love, we must of necessity maintain a spirit of reciprocity, and love Him as we are admonished in the Bible, and that is: "And thou shalt love the Lord thy God with all thine heart, and with all thy soul, and with all thy might" (Deut. 6:5).

It is a foregone conclusion that we do not deserve His love, nor can we earn it or pay for it, but we are to receive it and respond to it by worshipping and serving Him in love. John was inspired to write: "We love Him because He first loved us" (1 John 4:19). Not only do we love Him because he first loved us, but we love Him because of who He is and because of what He has done, is doing and plans to accomplish in the future ages. Our love expresses itself in service and increases as our ministry becomes more effective.

It is because of divine, love, mercy, grace, righteousness and power, the servants of the Lord are able to succeed in the ministry our Lord has called us to. That leaves no room for foolish boasting within ourselves, or developing a case of personal aggrandizement, for He alone is worthy of all praise and glory, for the work He accomplishes through His obedient servants. However, we need not be ashamed of that which our Lord chooses to accomplish.

All of our Lord's servants will not rule over nations on the New Earth as kings, nor will all serve as priests. Some may rule over ten cities and some over five, but all who qualify, according to our Lord's eternal standards, will be appointed to positions that He chooses for them, as He wills. He tells us: "And the city had no need of the sun, neither of the moon, to shine in it: for the glory of the Lord did lighten it, and the Lamb is the light thereof. And the nations of them that are saved shall walk in the light of it: and the kings of the earth do bring their glory and honor into it" (Rev. 21:23,24).

There will be no room for petty jealousies, competition and compromising politics in our Lord's kingdom. His servants will be entirely satisfied with their appointments and will humbly serve as the Holy Spirit directs. Little boys love to play with their toy automobiles and little girls with their dolls. God's spiritual babies will have their toys and be happy with them. Spiritual adults are not satisfied to play with toys. They have graduated beyond that stage in their growth toward maturity.

Our heavenly Bridegroom will thus appoint His loyal subjects to the positions, in our Father's eternal kingdom, to which His servants are well qualified to fill, by His grace, and not within themselves alone. To aspire to any special position, for which we are not fully qualified, can only result in disappointment. Valuable lessons, well learned in this life, will assist in proper preparation.

Jesus said, "This is my commandment, That ye love one another, as this have loved you" (John 15:12). The love of our heavenly Bridegroom for His bride, is to be equaled by her love for Him. Only divine love can accomplish this. He loved us enough to lay down His life for us. Do we love Him enough to lay down our lives for Him, and for others that they may experience the joys of salvation? What have we, as individuals, invested in the kingdom?

As the years come and go, there is a tendency on the part of God's people to reminisce and focus their minds upon past accomplishments. How much better it is to train our minds to concentrate on future events, which are soon to be revealed in reality. As the Apostle Paul wrote: "Brethren, I count not myself to have apprehended: but this one thing I do, forgetting those things which are behind, and reaching forth unto those things which are before, I press toward the mark for the prize of the high calling of God in Christ Jesus" (Phil. 3:13,14).

There will be no misfits in God's eternal, literal kingdom. All who are appointed to positions of honor and responsibility will be well fitted for those positions. It is quite obvious that there are misfits in the present Christian community. Some endeavoring to preach the Gospel of Christ who have never been born of the Spirit. Many called to evangelize who have chosen to minister in other ways, due perhaps to a lack of faith. The Bible says, "For the gifts and calling of God are without repentance" (Romans 11:29). A God-called servant may turn from the Lord for a period of time, but when he is restored to fellowship, the call confronts him and to enjoy a right relationship with the Father, he must respond to the call and be obedient.

Men make decisions, some good and some bad, but God keeps accurate records and will reward all of His servants according to our works, our motives, our opportunities, and whether or not His will has been accomplished.

The Bride of Christ and Her Maidens

God, our heavenly Father, in His infinite love and wisdom, has pronounced a special blessing upon those who are called to the marriage supper of the Lamb, as the Bible says: "Let us be glad and rejoice, and give honor to Him: for the marriage of the Lamb is come, *and His wife has made herself ready.* And to her was granted that she should be arrayed in fine linen, clean and bright, for the fine linen is the righteous ACTS of the saints.

Then he said to me, Write: Blessed are those who are CALLED to the marriage supper of the Lamb! And he said to me, These are the true sayings of God" (Rev. 19:7–9).

There are two special statements included in the above verses, which must captivate our attention, namely: One; "His wife (bride) has made herself ready." This requires works, special preparation, necessary qualifications.

Two; "Blessed are those who are called." He implies that all are not called to the marriage supper.

For example, infant babies are seldom called to attend special functions, such as banquets, etc. They are not old enough to appreciate such special celebrations. So it is in God's kingdom. Many believers have never grown beyond the stages of spiritual infancy. They are in the kingdom, will be in the rapture, but are not qualified to participate in special functions that are designed for those who are spiritually mature.

As there were spiritual babies in the early church, there are spiritual babies in the modern-day church. In Paul's letter to the church at Corinth, he addressed this situation in the following words: "And I, brethren, could not speak to you as to spiritual people but as to carnal, as to babes in Christ. I have fed you with milk, and not with meat: for hitherto ye were not able to bear it, neither yet now are ye able" (1 Cor. 3:1,2). They were in Christ, but still in their infancy.

The marriage supper of the Lamb may indeed be classified as heaven's most glorious celebration the end of this age, and is included in the consummation of our Lord's ministry of reconciliation. What a magnificent event for God's people to look forward to, and that will certainly be the beginning of even greater things to come.

Good works that the Lord accomplishes through His dedicated, mature servants, are even now qualifying many who are to be included in the Bride of Christ. We are convinced, by the Word, that all believers in the church, the body of Christ, will not be a part of the Bride. Positions in the Bride of Christ will be determined by our Lord at the judgment of rewards, which will take place in heaven, while the tribulation is in progress on earth. At that time, each of the Lord's servants, will be rewarded according to their works. Rewards will be given commensurate to service rendered, according to the parable Jesus gives us as recorded in Luke 19:11–26.

It is not a mere assumption to believe that those who have produced no acceptable works in the sight of God are to be excluded from the Bride of Christ. They have failed to make themselves ready, by divine grace, and their works are destroyed, as the Bible tells us: "Now if anyone builds on this foundation with gold, silver, precious stones, wood, hay, straw, each one's work will become clear; for the Day will declare it, because it will be revealed by fire; and the fire will test every one's work, of what sort it is. If anyone's work which he has built on it endures, he will receive a reward. If anyone's work is burned, he will suffer loss; but he himself will be saved, yet so as by fire" (1 Cor. 3:12–15).

Many of the works that professing Christians are producing

in our day are undoubtedly being categorized as wood, hay, and straw, combustible materials that do not remain.

In consideration of various Bible references, we therefore conclude that positions in the Bride of Christ are reserved for those mature believers who meet His requirements. However, it is also a fact that all of God's people, from the spiritual infants to mature servants, will be ecstatically happy in heaven and God's eternal kingdom, for there will be no sorrow there.

Those who enter His eternal kingdom, as spiritual babies, will have ample time to grow, develop, and assume certain responsibilities, as our Lord appoints and directs. In His increasing and expanding government and kingdom, new positions will open up and qualified servants will occupy them, under the direction of the Holy Spirit. God does all things well and His ways are perfect.

All do not have the same ability or stability, so each will be selected proportionately in accordance with their qualifications. Many surprises await the children of God, and when we are ushered from this life into that most glorious future, millions of astonished Christians will experience a momentary remorse, for our failure to take advantage of God-given opportunities. Now is the time to acquire the ability to move progressively forward in the divine rhythm and learn to not only "live in the realm of the Spirit" but also to "walk in the Spirit." The spiritual life involves more than a mere profession of Christianity, although that too is extremely important, for it is the beginning of greater things to come.

Vivid examples in the Word of God, as well as living examples in our day, speak to us of the necessity for embracing the lifestyle set forth by our Lord Jesus Himself, and especially in His great message as delivered on the Mount, and recorded in Matthew chapters 5,6, and 7. Yes, in all truth, the Beatitudes express His will for His people, and obedience to His word can only result in good.

Beautiful prophecies are given in the Old Testament concerning the relationship that is to exist between our heavenly Bridegroom and His Bride. Consider the following references as indicative of that which is to come:

"So Esther was taken unto King Ahasuerus into his house royal in the tenth month, which is the month Tabeth, in the seventh year of his reign. And the king loved Esther above all the women, and she obtained grace and favor in his sight more than all the virgins; so that he set the royal crown upon her head and made her queen instead of Vashti" (Esther 2:16,17).

King Ahasuerus did not take the entire group of virgins to serve as his queen, but only the one who met his expectations. Christ alone, our heavenly Bridegroom, is well qualified to select that segment of His body to serve as His Bride.

The Bride of Christ will have her maidens, or bridesmaids, beautifully prepared and attired for the great marriage supper. The Psalmist David, by special inspiration, gives us a beautiful prophecy concerning this grand event, when he wrote: "The king's daughter is all glorious WITHIN: her clothing is of wrought gold. She shall be brought unto the king in raiment of needlework: the virgins her companions that follow her shall be brought unto thee. With gladness and rejoicing shall they be brought: They shall enter into the king's palace" (Psalm 45:13–15).

NOTE: Later in this study, we refer to the ten virgins and also the 144,000 virgins.

King Solomon was well qualified to write of love. In the "SONG OF SOLOMON," certain passages contain definite prophetic significance, such as the following verses: "He brought me to the banqueting house, and his banner over me was love. My beloved spake, and said unto me, Rise up, my love, my fair one, and come away" (chapter 2:4,10).

Isaiah the prophet also gives us a glimpse of the beautiful relationship that will exist between the bridegroom and His bride. It is a word picture of complete blessing, for he writes: "I will greatly rejoice in the Lord, my soul shall be joyful in my God; for He has clothed me with the garments of salvation, He has covered me with the robe of righteousness, as a bridegroom decketh himself with ornaments, and as a bride adorneth herself with her jewels" (Isaiah 61:10).

There have been numerous interpretations and opinions concerning the ten virgins we read about in Matthew 25:1–10. Five of the virgins were wise, because they had extra oil in their vessels. The other five were foolish because their lamps went out, for their supply of oil was exhausted. The most convincing interpretation that I have heard about is as follows:

Virgins represent the Orthodox Jewish people who adhere to certain standards of morality. Their lamps typify their religious profession. The oil signifies the spiritual motivation within their lives. The wise virgins represent that segment of the Jewish nation that will receive Christ as their Messiah and Savior during the first three and one half years of the seven-year tribulation period. The foolish virgins are those who fail to receive Christ in time to go in the rapture of the 144,000, as the 144,000, raptured in the midst of the seven-year period are virgins, and will be caught up to heaven, as symbolized by the manchild in Revelation 12 and the 144,000 as referred to in Revelation 14.

Primarily, the lesson of the ten virgins provides an important lesson in preparation for the coming of Christ, but in a deeper sense also prophecy pertaining to the religious segment of Israel. All pieces of this prophetical jigsaw puzzle fit together perfectly and the picture is true.

Consider further the prophetical material offered to us in the following statement: "Then shall the kingdom of heaven be likened unto ten virgins, which took their lamps and went forth to meet the bridegroom" (Matt. 25:1).

Our word "THEN" signifies certain events following the prophecies in chapter 24 that are to be fulfilled during the seven-year period. The rapture of the church, as the great concluding event of the Gentile church age, will have taken place. The two witnesses, Moses and Elijah, representing the law and the prophets, will minister on earth for three and one half years, in Israel. The 144,000 will be converted and sealed in their foreheads and raptured in the midst of the seven-year period. They are virgins, according to Revelation 14:1–4. Could it be that the five wise virgins who make it into heaven for the marriage supper, and the 144,000 virgins, represent the same body of believers who are to be sealed from the nation of Israel?

Both prophecies could refer to the same event. In Revelation 7:4, we read where the 144,000 are sealed. In chapter 12 the man-child is caught up to heaven symbolizing a group from Israel, and the 144,000 are seen in heaven with the Father's name written in their foreheads (Rev. 4:1). They are virgins in that they have not become contaminated with the pagan religions of their day. As believers in Christ, they have received the Holy Spirit in a work of regeneration. They are the first fruits unto God from the restored Nation of Israel.

The second rapture is for the benefit of the 144,000 Jewish believers, sealed from the tribes of Israel. They are to occupy a prominent place in the kingdom of God, for the Word states: "These are they which follow the Lamb whithersoever He goeth" (Rev. 14:4b).

To teach one rapture only is truly a misinterpretation of related prophecy. The seven-year period is time to be allotted primarily to God's work of spiritual restoration in Israel.

Some additional information relative to the woman and man-child may be helpful. Various interpretations have been presented concerning this heavenly scene. Bear in mind that this scene is fulfilled during the seven-year period, and it symbolizes certain major events in Israel, as the following passage indicates:

> And there appeared a great wonder in heaven: a woman clothed with the sun, and the moon beneath her feet, and upon her head a crown of twelve stars: And she being with child cried, travailing in birth, and pained to be delivered. And she brought forth a man

child, who was to rule all nations with a rod of iron: and her child was caught up to God, and to His throne (Rev. 12:1,2,5).

The woman symbolizes Israel, as indicated by the crown of twelve stars, representing the twelve tribes of Israel. The sun symbolizes the light and warmth of the Gospel of Christ, and the moon beneath her feet represents the law. Her birth pains symbolize the birth pains of Israel as the 144,000 are born into the kingdom of God, through their acceptance of Christ Jesus as Messiah and Savior.

The manchild, symbolizing a segment of the nation of Israel, converted prior to the middle of the seven-year period, undoubtedly represents the 144,000, as they are the only group to be raptured in the middle of the seven-year period. They are to follow the Lord. Their childhood is indicative of their recent birth into the family of God, as newborn babes in Christ. Overcomers from the Thyatira church period will be categorized with them, as the Bible states: "And he that overcometh and keepeth my works unto the end, to him will I give power over the nations: And he shall rule them with a rod of iron; . . ." (Rev. 2:26,27a).

In all of the Lord's messages to the churches, He promised rewards to the overcomers. There will be much to overcome on earth, and especially while the tribulation is in progress.

It is believed by many Bible scholars that the "manchild" symbolizes that segment of the body of Christ, namely the 144,000 sealed out of the tribes of Israel, that are to serve also among His personal representatives throughout the universe. To teach that the manchild is Christ Himself would be to ignore various prophecies related to the woman and her offspring. This great event will transpire on earth during the first half of the tribulation period and not 2,000 years ago when Christ was born. His was a literal birth and Revelation 12 is providing prophetical information concerning a symbolical birth.

Christ as King of kings and Lord of lords will exercise supreme authority over all subordinates, as the prophecy tells us: "And the Lord shall be king over all the earth: in that day shall there be one Lord, and His name one" (Zechariah 14:9).

Those who qualify to serve as kings, over nations on the New Earth and on into the future eternity, shall be appointed by the Lord and shall serve under His supervision, as He tells us: "And from Jesus Christ, who is the faithful witness, and the first begotten of the dead, and the prince of the kings of the earth. Unto Him that loved us, and washed us from our sins in His own blood, And hath made us kings and priests unto God and His Father; to Him be glory and dominion forever and ever. Amen" (Rev. 1:5,6).

Kings and priests are made, not born. God our heavenly Father will make them and qualify them for their eternal positions, as they maintain their humility and dedication to the service He requires in this life. In plain words, His servants are either qualifying themselves, or disqualifying themselves, for promotions in the future life. It is all by the grace of God. What are you doing about it?

How rewarding it will be to hear Him say, "Come up higher, good and faithful servant, enter into the joys of your Lord."

Many born-again believers have failed to grow spiritually, into a state of spiritual maturity, as described in Hebrews 5:12, which reads: "For when for the time you ought to be teachers, you have need that one teach you again the first principles of the oracles of God; and you have come to require milk instead of solid food" (Weymouth).

All born-again, spiritually progressive believers, will be raptured prior to the beginning of the seven-year period, which is the seventieth week of years allotted to the nation of Israel for the purpose of accomplishing their spiritual restoration to divine fellowship, according to the prophecy as recorded (Daniel 9:24–27).

Lukewarm professing Christians will not qualify, spiritually, to be in the first rapture; neither will they qualify to be raptured with the 144,000 Jewish believers, who are to be raptured in the middle of the seven-year period, but when they are moved out of their comfort zone, and face the horrendous plagues in the last three and one half years, they will undoubtedly experience a spiritual renewal, and thus qualify for the third rapture.

Read Revelation 7:9–17. This passage speaks of the great multitude of people who have cleansed their robes in the blood of the Lamb and are to be taken up out of great tribulation. The Scriptures do not indicate that they die, or are resurrected, but they will be seen in heaven, so it is concluded that there will be a third rapture near the end of the great tribulation.

Another resurrection will occur at the beginning of the Millennium, as the prophecy states: "And I saw thrones, and they sat upon them, and judgement was given unto them: and I saw the souls of them that were beheaded for the witness of Jesus, and for the Word of God, and which had not worshipped the beast, neither his image, neither had received his mark upon their foreheads, or in their hands" . . . (Rev. 20:4).

In prayerful consideration of these and other related Bible passages, we come to the conclusion that God has set forth in Scriptures certain qualifications, which must be met by those whom He will choose to comprise the Bride.

The following standards of true Bible holiness must be taken into consideration, namely:

"And be not drunk with wine, wherein is excess; but be filled with the Spirit" (Eph. 5:18).

"If we live in the Spirit, let us also walk in the Spirit" (Gal. 5;25).

"For as many as are led by the Spirit of God, they are the sons of God" (Rom. 8:14).

We therefore see five essential Bible qualifications for a position in the Bride of Christ, but they do not necessarily guarantee that all who are thus qualified will be chosen to share in the exalted position. They are as follows:

1. A genuine born-again experience.

2. A Spirit-filled life.
3. A Spirit-led life.
4. A spiritually mature life.
5. A spiritually productive life.

Remember Jesus said, "Herein is my Father glorified, that you bear much fruit; so shall you be My disciples" (John 15:7). The fruit of a banana tree is bananas; the fruit of an apple tree is apples; the fruit of an orange tree is oranges, and the fruit of a Christian is Christians. If we are not occupied in helping to win souls, we are fruitless.

All are not called to preach, teach, sing or play a musical instrument, but all are called to witness. God calls some to a ministry of intercessory prayer and calls others to a ministry of giving, but all of God's people should be involved one way or another in His great soul-winning ministry of redemption.

Types and Shadows of This Event

Major events, which have transpired during the Church Age, were prophesied of in the Old Testament and fulfilled in the New. Bible prophecies are being fulfilled on a daily basis. God inspired Daniel the prophet to write of certain events that were to be fulfilled in the end time, and they are in the process of fulfillment in our day.

Daniel did not understand the meaning of certain prophecies, which he wrote, as inspired by the Holy Spirit, so inquired of the Lord, as the Bible states: "And I heard, but I understood not: then said I, O my Lord, what shall be the end of these things? And He said, Go thy way, Daniel: for the words are closed and sealed till the time of the end. Many shall be purified, and made white, and tried; but the wicked shall do wickedly; and none of the wicked shall understand; but the wise shall understand" (Dan. 12:8–10).

Daniel also wrote: "And they that be wise shall shine as the brightness of the firmament; and they that turn many to righteousness as the stars forever and ever. But thou, O Daniel, shut up the words, and seal the book, even to the time of the end: many shall run to and fro, and knowledge shall be increased" (Dan. 12:3,4).

We are now living in the time of the end, and God has opened the book for His people to understand the prophecies recorded in the Book of Daniel. Knowledge is increasing at an unprecedented rate, in all areas of human understanding. Along with all other branches of learning, there is also increasing spiritual illumination concerning God's will and Word. "He that hath an ear, let him hear what the Spirit saith unto the churches" (Rev. 2:7,11,17,29; 3:6,13,22).

Interpretations of Bible prophecy, as presented fifty years ago, have changed drastically. Would-be prophets preached soul-stirring messages in the thirties that were proven to be unscriptural later on, but the Word has not changed. God's people must maintain open minds and open hearts to receive fresh spiritual understanding.

The Old Testament records certain prototypes, or types and shadows of that which is to come, and many of them are being fulfilled during this period of divine administration. Others are yet to be fulfilled on into the future.

Have you ever questioned God as to why He chose to cause a deep sleep to fall on Adam, and then remove a rib from Adam's side while he slept? With the rib, a segment of Adam's body, God created a bride for the first Adam. So Mrs. Adam was created from better material than her husband.

Could it be that through God's foreknowledge He planned this special creation of Eve, as a type or foreshadow, of even a greater creation, namely a bride for Christ, the second Adam? The Bible tells us: "And so it is written, The first man Adam was made a living soul; the last Adam was made a quickening Spirit" (1 Cor. 15:45).

Is it possible to believe that as God removed a segment of Adam's body and created a bride for him, so the Holy Spirit is in the process of separating a segment of the body of Christ and creating a Bride for Christ?

Why not consider other types from the Old Testament that are applicable to the New? How about Abraham's decision in the selection of a bride for Isaac? Abraham is a type of God our heavenly Father; Isaac, his son, is a type of our Lord Jesus Christ, God the Son; and Eliezer, Abraham's steward or head servant, typifies the Holy Spirit. In obedience to the will and command of Abraham, Eliezer went to Abraham's family to select a bride for Isaac. He went prayerfully and the Lord directed in the selection. In answer to the servant's prayer, Rebecca appeared at the well, granted his request for a drink of water, and voluntarily offered to water the camels also. Those who are qualifying themselves, by divine grace, to occupy positions in the Bride of Christ, have learned to render voluntary service.

Rebecca received special gifts and was a special person.

Eliezer gave valuable gifts to the members of the family, but special gifts to Rebecca. The Holy Spirit is imparting gifts to the members of the body of Christ, but special gifts to those whom He is separating to comprise the Bride.

Rebecca made the right choice: "And they called Rebecca, and said unto her, wilt thou go with this man? And she said, I will go" (Gen. 24:58). It was in her power to choose whether or not she would become Isaac's bride. We too have the power of choice. We choose whether or not we will make a total surrender of our will to God, or not. The journey was rough, but culminated in a successful union.

Another interesting love story is recorded in the Book of Ruth. The widow, Ruth, a pagan in the land of Moab, made a historical decision when she said to Naomi, her mother-in-law: "Intreat me not to leave thee, or to return from following after thee: for where thou goest, I will go, and where thou lodgest, I will lodge: thy people shall be my people, and thy God my God: Where thou diest, I will die, and there will I be buried: the Lord do so to me, and more also, if ought but death part thee and me" (Ruth 1:16,17).

Ruth had no children by her first husband, Naomi's son. Orpah, Naomi's other daughter-in-law, chose to remain in Moab and worship her pagan gods, but Ruth made the right choice, even though it meant separating herself from her own people and their gods.

The following sequence of events, in the life of Ruth, resulted in a beautiful romance and the name of "RUTH," the Gentile bride of Boaz, is included in the genealogy as recorded in Matthew 1:5. Great honor, in the life of Ruth, resulted from her decision to worship and serve the true God. In submission to her mother-in-law, she became the bride of Boaz, the lord of the harvest.

Ruth labored, voluntarily, from morning until evening in the harvest field, gleaning grain for Naomi and herself. Boaz, a relative of Naomi, observed the young lady, was impressed by her, and gave instructions to the young men to "drop handfuls on purpose." He also encouraged Ruth to continue gleaning in his fields until the end of the harvest. We have a beautiful example of voluntary, industrious labor.

Boaz, the lord of the harvest, is a type of Christ. Naomi, a type of the Holy Spirit, "one sent alongside to help," and Ruth, a type of the bride of Christ. As Ruth obeyed the instructions of Naomi, she was led into a beautiful and productive marriage with Boaz, and became the great-grandmother of King David. In submission to Naomi's instructions, Ruth said, "All that thou sayest unto me I will do" (Ruth 3:5). As believers in Christ, we say, "Not my will but your will be done."

In preparation for Heaven's Most Glorious Celebration, the Holy Spirit is imparting special Gifts of the Spirit and demonstrating the fruit of the Spirit, in and through the lives of His dedicated, spiritually mature, and spiritually productive servants. Spiritual babes are not sufficiently knowledgeable in the operation of the gifts of the Spirit to be thus used of the Lord.

When divine love is operating within the lives of believers, and through the lives of believers, there will be no evil reports, scandalous criticisms, or demonically inspired judgments, but harmony and a unified relationship will prevail. As God's servants learn to practice Christian ethics, sowing good seed, refusing to show partiality, but demonstrating sincere love toward all, believers in Christ, unity in the Spirit and in the Word will develop more and more, toward that glorious, unified relationship with Christ Jesus our Lord and King. Why waste time in useless works? God wants His people to increase in love and knowledge.

God requires holiness and purity of heart, on the part of all who choose to live in that inner-circle relationship with Him. He tells us: "Seeing you have purified your souls in obeying the truth through the Spirit unto unfeigned love of the brethren, see that you love one another with a pure heart fervently" (1 Peter 1:22).

Isaiah the prophet speaks of the bride's adornments, as follows: "I will greatly rejoice in the Lord, my soul shall be joyful in my God; for he hath clothed me with the garments of salvation, he hath covered me with the robe of righteousness, as a bridegroom decketh himself with ornaments, and as a bride adorneth herself with her jewels" (Isa. 61:10).

"The joy of the Lord is your strength" (Nehemiah 8:10). God's people are joyful in the Lord because we have salvation and have been made righteous. The adornment that pleases the Lord is an inner beauty, described by the Apostle Peter in the following words: "Whose adorning let it not be that outward adorning of plaiting the hair, and of wearing of gold, or of putting on of apparel; But let it be the hidden man of the heart, in that which is not corruptible, even the ornament of a meek and quiet spirit, which is in the sight of God of great price" (1 Peter 3:3,4).

As the Christian wife is to honor her Christian husband, and be submissive to his headship in the family, so are those who will constitute the bride of Christ learning to be totally submissive to the will of Christ Jesus.

It is not enough to call Him Lord, but we are to serve and honor Him as our Lord.

After ministering in remote areas of the Philippines some years ago for a three-week period, and living under primitive conditions, I returned to Manila. A missionary friend volunteered the information as he said, "I could not minister under those conditions, as you do."

The Marriage Supper and Home
of the Bride

The parable given by our Lord, as recorded in Matthew 22:1–10, has very special significance. Of all parables given us by Jesus Himself, this particular parable is undoubtedly related to the marriage of the Lamb. Jesus said, "The kingdom of heaven is like to a certain king, which made a marriage for his son." His reference to servants and guests suggests to us that others will be in attendance at the great marriage supper in addition to our heavenly bridegroom, the bride, her maidens, and also guests and servants.

Inasmuch as the marriage of the Lamb is the most important marriage celebration referred to in the Bible, it is obvious that the parable provides us with a degree of information relative to so great an event.

Jesus gave us other parables, especially related to the kingdom of heaven, as the record states: "Behold a sower went forth to sow"; "The kingdom of heaven is likened unto a man which sowed good seed in his field"; "The kingdom of heaven is like to a grain of mustard seed, which a man took and sowed in his field"; "The kingdom of heaven is like unto leaven, which a woman took, and hid in three measures of meal, till the whole was leavened"; "Again the kingdom of heaven is like unto treasure hid in a field"; "Again the kingdom of heaven is like unto a merchant man, seeking goodly pearls"; "And again, the kingdom of heaven is like unto a net, that was cast into the sea, and gathered of every kind": (Matt. 13: portions of verses 3,24,31,33,44,45,47).

When the disciples interrogated Jesus, desiring to know why

He spoke in parables, He replied: "Because it is given unto you to know the mysteries of the kingdom of heaven, but to them it is not given." Jesus did not reveal the mysteries of the kingdom of heaven to unbelievers. He used the commonplace things of life as illustrations.

In the parable of the marriage, the king sent forth servants to invite guests to this very special occasion, but they rejected the invitation. The king then sent forth other servants and their invitation was made light of and they were mistreated and slain. The king therefore was angry and sent judgment upon the murderers and burned their city. After that the servants were sent forth to invite any who would come, both bad and good. On one occasion Jesus said, "Verily I say unto you, that the publicans and harlots go into the kingdom of God before you" (Matt. 21:31b). Spiritual babes are contented and happy with their toys. Mature believers have laid aside their toys and accepted greater things.

Our capacity to fully enjoy the glorious realities of the heavenly home is determined, in part, by the degree of service rendered in this present life. Remember, the sowers went forth to sow, according to the parable given by our Lord and some enjoyed a greater harvest, as the Bible says: "But other fell into good ground, and brought forth fruit, some an hundredfold, some sixtyfold, and some thirtyfold" (Matt. 13:8).

The body of Christ is referred to in the male gender and the bride of Christ in the female gender. We are providing some references on the following page. Just as God did not use the entire body of Adam with which to create the bride for Adam, so the Holy Spirit is not using the entire body of Christ with which to prepare a bride for Christ.

The question is: Are we to conclude that all of the guests, and all of the servants, including the bridesmaids, as referred to in Psalm 45:14, are to constitute the bride of Christ or only that number selected by the Holy Spirit and qualified according to the

King's standards and not man's? And we must also consider the status of the millions of spiritual babes, born again but still babes, unable to accept responsibility in the kingdom until they grow to spiritual maturity.

Born-again believers in Christ constitute the body of Christ, the church, for the Scripture says, "Now you are the body of Christ, and members in particular" (1 Cor. 12:27). Taking out membership in a local church or denomination does not necessarily indicate that we are members of the body of Christ. Going into a chicken house does not make you a chicken, or entering a garage does not suddenly transform you into an automobile, so neither does entering a church make you a child of God. Many people throng into church buildings who have never received Christ as their personal Savior and Lord.

Christ is the head of His body, the church, as the Bible says, "And He is the head of the body, the church: who is the beginning, the firstborn from the dead; that in all things He might have the preeminence" (Col. 1:18).

It is the will of God for a state of spiritual unity to prevail among all believers in Christ, but that may not be accomplished until the Millennial reign. Due to man-made barriers between Christian denominations, there continues to be much carnality, competition, compromise, sectarianism and other hindrances that cause strife, confusion and division.

The Bible tells us: And he gave some, apostles, and some, prophets; and some evangelists; and some, pastors and teachers; For the perfecting of the saints, for the work of the ministry, for the edifying of the body of Christ: Till we all come in the unity of the faith, and of the knowledge of the Son of God, unto a perfect (mature) man, unto the measure of the stature of the fullness of Christ: that we henceforth be no more children, tossed to and fro, and carried about with every wind of doctrine, by the sleight of men, and cunning craftiness, whereby they lie in wait to deceive; But speak the truth in love, may grow up into Him in all things, which is the head, even Christ (Eph. 4:11–15).

Obedience to the call of God is essential.

God pronounced a very special blessing when He said, "Blessed are they which are called unto the marriage supper of the Lamb. And he said unto me, these are the true sayings of God" (Rev. 19:9).

Our English word "BLESSED" is translated from the Greek word "MAKARIOS," meaning to be supremely blessed, over and above ordinary blessings. Our English words, bless, blessed, blessing, and blessedness, in the form of verbs, adjectives, and nouns, have been translated from seven different Greek words, implying various stages of blessing.

The Greek word "MAKARIOS," translated into our English word "BLESSED" has been used only in a few references in the New Testament (Matt. 5:3–7); (Luke 6:20–22); seven times in Revelation, and a limited number of references pertaining to very special blessings, for meeting certain conditions, as determined by the Lord Himself.

For example: "It is more blessed to give than to receive" (Acts 20:35c).

God desires to bless everyone, but many are unwilling, either deliberately or because of their ignorance of the Word, to meet His conditions and pay the price for greater blessings. The words "bless," "blessing," "blessed," and "blessedness," are used about 500 times in the Bible. But the words "curse" and "cursed" are used only 71 times. This suggests that God is more willing to bless than to curse, but when people refuse to obey His call and His Word, thus meeting His conditions, they invariably suffer His displeasure and judgment.

Could you imagine a bride walking down the aisle of a church, to be married to a fine, handsome young man, and yet she is not properly groomed or dressed? She has failed to make proper preparation for a very special event. Her appearance is ridiculous and embarrassing to the bridegroom, her family and the guests. Special preparation is essential for special events.

Some of us who consider ourselves to be spiritual giants, and well qualified to occupy positions of honor in our Lord's eternal kingdom, may suddenly discover that we are spiritual dwarfs in the sight of God. Others, in their depths of humility and sincerity, do not judge themselves to be worthy of special honor, so may experience certain unexpected surprises when the appointments are made.

Jesus tells us: "For whosoever exalteth himself shall be abased; and he that humbleth himself shall be exalted" (Luke 14:11).

The Bible also says; "A man's pride shall bring him low: but honor shall uphold the humble in spirit (Prov. 29:23).

It is commonly reported that some people are so humble they are proud of it.

God makes no mistakes and when He makes the appointments, He will select His servants according to their qualifications, so they will not function as misfits in the positions He has chosen for them. Only the precious blood of our Lord Jesus Christ can properly prepare our hearts and minds for the work our Lord desires to accomplish through us. None of us are sufficiently knowledgeable to decide our places of service in His kingdom, and it is best that we are not. We will learn His will for us at the Judgment of rewards. His decisions will be largely influenced by our records, our motives, our attitudes and our works.

In His great love, mercy, provision and power, He has made us righteous and given most of us a lifetime to develop and become familiar with the lifestyle of service that is in full accordance with His will and Word. If we fail to develop that lifestyle, we are the losers. God does not alter His plans and standards to correspond with ours. If our desires and personal plans are contrary to His, we must change. Any act of self-denial on our part, in bearing the cross He has chosen for us, can only lead to greater victories ahead.

Prophecies, pertaining to the Bride of Christ and her eternal home, indicate that the New Jerusalem will be her eternal place of abode. The Bible says: "And I John saw the holy city, the New Jerusalem, coming down from God out of heaven, prepared as a bride adorned for her husband" (Rev. 21:2). Talk about precious gems: The city will have streets of gold, the foundations garnished with gems, gates of pearl and such beauty of indescribable splendor that the inhabitants and all visitors will be made to marvel eternally.

One of the seven angels spoke to John and said, "Come hither, I will show you the bride, the Lamb's wife" (Rev. 21:9b). He showed him the city. Some teach that the literal city is the bride. Others teach that it will not be a literal city. There is no indication in the context that it is a symbolical city. Every description he offers indicates that it will indeed be a literal city and will function on the new earth as a great metropolis and governmental center of the universe.

Therefore we conclude that the bride without the city will have no home, and the city without the bride would not be complete. Is it impossible to believe that His bride will inhabit the city when it descends from heaven to the New Earth?

All members of the body of Christ are not to live in the New Jerusalem, but only those who are to be placed there as included in the bride and others whom the Lord may select to serve in positions for which He has qualified them.

Nations of the redeemed will inhabit the New Earth and kings will reign over them. The Bible says; "And the nations of them that are saved shall walk in the light of it: and the kings of the earth do bring their glory and honor into it" (Rev. 21:24). When God's people arrive on the New Earth, we will undoubtedly exclaim! "The half has not been told."

The dimensions and other descriptive information, concerning the literal New Jerusalem, is provided for our understanding (Rev. 21:10–27).

The present earth is not to be utterly destroyed and go into oblivion, but will simply be renovated by fire and made new. The Bible states that the earth perished in the days of Noah: "Whereby the world that then was, being overflowed with water, perished (2 Peter 3:6).

He also tells us: "And God said to Noah, The end of all flesh is come before Me; for the earth is filled with violence through them; and behold, I will destroy them with the earth" (Gen. 6:13). The earth was not destroyed, to the extent that it ceased to exist, but was thoroughly cleansed by water.

It will be cleansed again at the end of the Millennial reign, and this time by fire, but the same planet will be renewed and restored to its original state of beauty and productivity. Paradise shall indeed be restored.

Jesus said, "Blessed are the meek: for they shall inherit the earth" (Matt. 5:5). The Bible also tells us: "While the earth remaineth, seedtime and harvest, and cold and heat, and summer and winter, and day and night shall not cease" (Gen. 22).

The Bible says, "And I saw a new heaven and a new earth: for the first heaven and the first earth were passed away; and there was no more sea" (Rev. 21:1). We understand that the present earth will thus pass from one state to another and be totally renewed. Even as Christians have become a new creation, for the Word says, "If any man be in Christ, he is a new creature: old things are passed away; behold all things are become new" (2 Cor. 5:17). We live in the same body, but the inner person has become alive, a new, born-again believer in Christ. Without Christ people are dead, spiritually speaking. So the earth will be reborn.

Nations of redeemed humans, along with nations of angelic beings, will continue to live, love, worship and serve God, in a beautiful, utopian existence, on the new earth and in the new heavens. Successive generations will transfer to other planets, solar systems and galaxies, on into the eternal future. Is this impossible to believe? With God all things are possible and with Him all things are perfect.

Jesus said; "And, behold, I come quickly; and my reward is with Me, to give every man according at his work shall be. I am Alpha and Omega, the beginning and the end, the first and the last.

"BLESSED are they that do His commandments, that they may have right to the tree of life, and may enter in through the gates into the city" (Rev. 22:12–14).

The Holy Spirit is speaking to the churches, and as believers, we are admonished to keep our spiritual ears open and be prepared to listen to what He is saying.

The Word declares: "But as it is written, Eye hath not seen, nor ear heard, neither have entered into the heart of man, the things which God hath prepared for them that love Him. But God hath revealed them unto us by His Spirit: for the Spirit searcheth all things, yea, THE DEEP THINGS OF GOD" (1 Cor. 2:9,10).

Shared, spiritual illumination, as revealed by the Holy Spirit, and authenticated by the Word of God, serves to increase the faith of believers and to result in increasing spiritual victories. If that is not our goal in life, what is?

NOTE: I personally consider the regular *King James Version* of the Bible to be the most authentic Bible in print, but I also use the NKJV and certain other versions part time, because of the modern English. However, the KJV and the NKJV were used mainly in this series of studies.

Appendix A

Supplementary Questions and Answers

QUESTION: Does not the Bible refer to the church, or body of Christ, as the Bride?

ANSWER: Not to my knowledge. If you know of such a references, please bring it to my attention. The Bible does tell us that we are married to Christ: "Wherefore, my brethren, ye also are become dead to the law by the body of Christ; that ye should be married to another, even to him who is raised from the dead, that we should bring forth fruit unto God" (Romans 7:4). Having been delivered from the law, through the death of Christ, we are free to be married to Christ and through an intimate relationship with Him, we are made productive. This is a spiritual union, but remember, spiritual babes do not reproduce.

QUESTION: Well, the Scripture does tell us that the husband is to love his wife even as Christ loves the church, does it not?

ANSWER: Yes, God intends for a beautiful relationship to exist between husband and wife, and also between Christ and the members of His body. He tells us: "Wives, submit yourselves unto your own husbands, as unto the Lord. For the husband is the head of the wife, even as Christ is the head of the church: and he is the savior of the body" (Eph. 5:22,23).

It is also a fact that just as some wives refuse to be totally submissive to their husbands, so many Christians fail to be totally submissive to the headship of Christ. It is quite apparent that many young couples rush into marriage prematurely, and consequently experience major adjustment problems. This is also true in the lives of many Christians, and as a result, there will be much stumbling and falling before they learn to walk.

QUESTION: Did not the Apostle Paul inform believers that he had betrothed them to one husband?

ANSWER: Yes. He said, "For I am jealous for you with godly jealousy. For I have betrothed you to one husband, that I may present you as a chaste virgin to Christ.

But I fear, lest somehow, as the serpent deceived Eve by his craftiness, so your minds may be corrupted from the simplicity that is in Christ" (2 Cor. 11:2,3).

Eve's conversation with the serpent resulted in their disobedience to the direct command of God, and subsequent banishment from the Garden of Eden.

When professing Christians persist in idle flirtations with the devil, their intimate relationship with Christ suffers.

Yes, as the Bible says: "Husbands, love your wives, even as Christ also loved the church, and gave Himself for it; That He might sanctify and cleanse it with the washing of water by the Word, That He might present it to Himself a glorious church, not having spot, or wrinkle, or any such thing; but that it should be holy and without blemish" (Eph. 5:25–27).

Yes, Jesus loves the church, every member of His body, but is it not highly probable that many members do not love Him as much as we should?

We know also that: "God so loved the world that He gave His only begotten Son, that whosoever believeth in Him should not perish, but have everlasting life" (John 3:16).

But, it is also a fact that the major part of earth's population does not love God.

Through careful, concentrated, and prayerful study of the Scriptures, the Holy Spirit provides increasing knowledge. May we give God our very best that we may receive His best, now and eternally.

God's Angel Messengers

Foreword

In this day when interest in angels is very intense, it is imperative that truth relative to their existence and purpose be shared, based on many scriptural accounts.

Angels are God's messengers to His people, and their ministry does not in any way disagree with the work and ministry of the Holy Spirit, or the Word of God.

I am concerned in this day of so-called New Age philosophy, when some people venerate angels in a fashion that borders on worship. The Bible warns us against worshiping the creature rather than the Creator (Rom. 1:24–25). Only Jesus Christ, God the Son, who is creator of all things and by whom all things consist, is worthy of our worship (Col. 1:17; 2:18).

Nor should we confuse angels, whether visible or invisible, with God the Holy Spirit, for He is the third person of the Trinity. Angels do not indwell men, seal them in redemption, or convict men of sin, righteousness, and judgment. This is the work of the Holy Spirit. The Holy Spirit reveals and interprets Jesus Christ to men.

There is a need for this book, more than ever, because of the emphasis on angels in these last days. I am confident that Dr. James B. Reesor's knowledge of the Scriptures, and many years of experience, qualifies him to correctly interpret the Bible references to angels, and explain their relationship and ministry to men. I consider it a personal privilege and honor to submit this foreword.

Rev. Floyd Myers, Pastor
Greencastle, PA 17225

Introduction

God's angels are ministering spirits, as we read: "Are they not all ministering spirits, sent forth to minister for them who shall be heirs of salvation?" (Heb. 1:14).

The fascinating study of angels tends to broaden our scope, increase our appreciation of God's creative power, stimulate our thirst for greater knowledge of God's most glorious plan for His eternal future, and deepen our dedication. The joy of placing the prophetical pieces of God's great jigsaw puzzle together, in their proper position, is incredible, as the Holy Spirit directs.

We hear and read much concerning angel activity in our day, where these created beings have suddenly appeared, communicated with humans, and then disappeared. Angels appeared to Mary, my wife, on two separate occasions. It is my prayer that the contents of this three-book volume will touch the hearts of unsaved men, women and children, and stimulate the faith of believers.

I hereby dedicate this book to Mary, also to our family members who have offered much encouragement, and also to our assistants, participating ministers, field representatives, partners and friends of BIBLE RESEARCH MINISTRIES, INC. We especially give thanks and praise to our Wonderful Lord, who called us to this outreach, soul-winning ministry in the Philippines.

Sincerely,

James B. Reesor

Angels as Created Beings

Angels are created beings, just as men are created beings. Angels were created long before men, and no doubt God created the different orders of angels near the beginning of His creation.

Our English word "angel" is translated from the Hebrew word "MAL'AK," pronounced "MAL-AWK." "Mal-awk" may be interpreted as: ambassador, angel, king, or messenger. Our words "angel" and "angels" are used approximately 290 times in the Bible.

In the New Testament, our word "angel" is translated from the Greek word "AGGELOS" or "ANG'ELOS," pronounced "ANG'-EL-OS," meaning angel or messenger.

God's loyal angels serve in various capacities, and we have many references to their activities as recorded in the Bible. The study of angels is indeed one of the most gratifying studies of the Bible, and we need to thank God regularly for the good work they accomplish under divine guidance. According to the Bible, they minister for believers. Notice what He said: "Are they not all ministering spirits, sent forth to minister for them who shall be heirs of salvation?" (Heb. 1:14).

Angels are spirit beings, just as humans are spirit beings. The Bible says: "Furthermore we have had fathers of our flesh which corrected us, and we gave them reverence: shall we not much rather be in subjection unto the Father of spirits, and live?" (Heb. 12:9). Read Hebrews 12:23 also.

Angels also have bodies, immortal bodies, and they eat food.

God fed the children of Israel in the wilderness manna, which is referred to as "angel food." "Man did eat angels' food" (Ps. 78:25a).

Two angels accompanied the Lord when they visited with Abraham. The Bible tells us: "And the Lord appeared unto him in the plains of Mam're: . . . And when he saw them, he ran to meet them from the tent door, and bowed himself toward the ground, And said, My Lord, if now I have found favor in thy sight, pass not away, I pray thee, from thy servant: Let a little water, I pray you, be fetched, and wash your feet, and rest yourselves under the tree: And I will fetch a morsel of bread, and comfort ye your hearts; after that ye shall pass on" (Gen. 1–8).

Abraham instructed Sarah to "make cakes upon the hearth." He ran and fetched a calf, had it butchered and provided meat, cakes, butter and milk for their meal, "and they did eat." We see many similarities between angelic sons of God and human sons of God. Then the Lord promised Abraham and Sarah a son. Sarah doubted, but the Lord said, "Is anything too hard for the Lord?" (verse 14). The Lord remained with Abraham, discussing the problem of Sodom and Gomorrah, because of their wickedness. The two angels went on to Sodom, arriving there in the evening and spent the night with Lot. Lot had a feast prepared for them; they ate the meal and then had an encounter with the evil men of Sodom, which resulted in judgment upon the wicked Sodomites, in the form of blindness (Gen. 19:1–11).

They had planned to lie down and rest, but their plans were altered because of the demonically inspired words and actions of the homosexuals.

Jesus said, "Likewise also as it was in the days of Lot; they did eat, they drank, they bought, they sold, they planted, they builded; But the same day that Lot went out of Sodom it rained fire and brimstone from heaven, and destroyed them all. Even thus shall it be in the day when the Son of man is revealed" (Luke 17:28–30).

Because of unbelief, violence, and rampant sin, God has sent destructive judgment time and again, and His angel messengers have carried out His will. Modern day nations that have chosen, by premeditation, to reject, resist, and openly defy God and rebel against Him and His people, shall certainly suffer the consequences of their willful unbelief and flagrant rejection of His love, mercy, grace, and righteousness.

Angels have been much in the news in recent years, with publications devoted to testimonials of people who have experienced angelic visitations. Even secular magazines have published articles, and there have undoubtedly been many UFO's seen and much additional evidence concerning places where they had landed.

Our one daughter, Jeanette, had an unusual experience. She and a friend were on a lake near Nashville, fishing, when they were attracted by an object hovering some distance above them. Jeanette, rather boldly, spoke aloud and said, "Hey you, if you are up there, come down and communicate with us." Nothing happened immediately, but a few minutes later, they started the motor on the boat and decided to try their luck in a different area.

As they started off, they were suddenly amazed to see a boat running along parallel to theirs, with no one at the controls, and a person standing in the boat dressed in a strange uniform. He did not speak with an audible voice, but he communicated very well. He said, "Young woman, you ought never to challenge we beings from outer space. Most of us are peace-loving beings, but there are some out there who would destroy you. You ought never to challenge us." He stopped communicating and disappeared as suddenly as he had appeared, boat and all.

Jeanette's friend said, "Jeanette, nothing happened. Don't ever tell anyone that we saw anything." Jeanette waited for two or three weeks and finally told us.

Certainly, with all available evidence, it would be ill advised to reject all belief in angels, UFO's, and interplanetary space travel, by angelic beings from outer space, and perhaps the Old

Testament resurrected saints may be more active than we think. We will be favorably impressed when we get to heaven and learn more about God's sons and daughters who have gone on before.

As has been often said, "The reality of the future is so much greater than our most vivid imagination, there is no comparison."

Mary, my wife, had two experiences with angels, according to her firm convictions. One was when we were pastoring a church at Tolstoy, South Dakota. I was away in a meeting, and she went to the church to pray. While praying an angel appeared and spoke to her. He was dressed in white with a light blue robe over the white clothing and said, "Do not fear, all is well." She had been concerned about the possibility of a move. After the angel spoke to her, he suddenly disappeared and she felt perfectly free from worry.

Her other experience was during a wedding reception at Lemmon, South Dakota, where we also pastored. The ladies were preparing lunch in the parsonage, when there was a knock at the back door. Mary went to investigate and a man was there, with peculiar attire, and requested some food. She went quickly, prepared food for him, and gave it to him. He thanked her profusely, and she sensed a heavenly presence. He turned and walked away.

Several ladies asked, "Who was that?" The man had totally disappeared. I walked around the house and he was nowhere in sight. He could not possibly have walked out of sight in about sixty seconds.

In times of extreme danger, including experiences that could only be interpreted as divine intervention, we were saved from what may easily have been critical accidents. We give praise to God and our thanks to our guardian angels. We have God's promise, in His Word: "The angel of the Lord encampeth round about them that fear Him, and delivereth them" (Ps. 34:7).

Isaiah also tells us: "So shall they fear (reverence) the name of the Lord from the west, and His glory from the rising of the sun.

When the enemy shall come in like a flood, the Spirit of the Lord shall lift up a standard against him" (Isa. 59:19).

Why risk our safety in the Lord by ignoring the safety rules He has established? When we love, respect, and obey God as we ought to, His precious promises will be fulfilled in our lives.

Fallen Angels

There are good angels and bad angels. We understand from the Scriptures that there were originally three archangels, namely, Michael, Gabriel, and Lucifer. One-third of the angels followed Lucifer, and his kingdom was Eden, which we refer to as planet Earth. According to the passage in Isaiah chapter fourteen, Lucifer reigned over nations of angelic beings, for the Scriptures state:

"How art thou fallen from heaven, O Lucifer, son of the morning! How art thou cut down to the ground, which didst weaken the nations! For thou hast said in thine heart, I will ascend into heaven, I will exalt my throne above the stars of God: I will sit also upon the mount of the congregation, in the sides of the north: I will ascend above the heights of the clouds; I will be like the most High" (Isa.14:12–14).

Certain Bible references suggest that the original name of this planet was "EDEN." Other planets are named, such as Mars, and Jupiter. Heaven is the name of the planet where God's throne is located.

Lucifer should have been contented, reigning over nations of angelic beings on the planet "Eden," but he became greedy, proud, and desired to become ruler of the universe, so he ascended into heaven, accompanied by his angelic host, to engage in warfare with God's loyal angels, and was defeated. He and his angels became fallen angels. Ezekiel the prophet gives us further insight into this event. He wrote as follows: "Thou has been in Eden the garden of God; every precious stone was thy covering, the sardius, topaz, and the diamond, the beryl, the onyx, and the jasper, the sapphire, the emerald, and the carbuncle, and gold: the workman-ship of thy tabrets and of thy pipes was prepared in thee in the day that thou was created" (Ezek. 28:13).

Ezekiel further tells us: "Thou art the anointed Cherub that covereth; and I have set thee so: thou was upon the holy mountain of God; thou hast walked up and down in the midst of the stones of fire (glittering lights reflected from the beautiful gems). Thou wast perfect in thy ways from the day thou wast created, till iniquity was found in thee" (Ezek. 28:14,15).

The context goes beyond the king of Tyre, and describes Lu-cifer very well. The earth is referred to as "Eden" in various places, for example: "I have made him fair by the multitude of his branches: so that all the trees of Eden, that were in the garden of God, envied him" (Ezek. 31:9). Also: "To whom art thou thus like in glory and in greatness among the trees of Eden? Yet shalt thou be brought down with the trees of Eden unto the nether parts of the earth: . . ." (Ezek. 31:18). The earth was called Eden in Genesis. God planted a garden eastward in Eden and placed man there (Gen. 2:8).

When Cain murdered his brother Abel, he went out from the presence of the Lord, and dwelt in the land of Nod, on the east of Eden (Gen. 4:16).

God also created the cherubim and seraphim. He created the seraphim with six wings. The Bible suggests that the cherubim had two wings. God also created an order of angelic beings with no wings. The Bible says: "Be not forgetful to entertain strangers: for thereby some have entertained angels unawares" (Heb. 13:2).

Only the angels that followed Lucifer in his rebellion became fallen angels. Jesus said, "I beheld satan as lightning fall from heaven" (Luke 10:18). Satan and his fallen angels will be involved in another war, during the tribulation, as the prophecy reads: "And there was war in heaven: Michael and his angels fought against the dragon; (satan) and the dragon fought and his angels, And prevailed not; neither was their place found any more in heaven" (Rev. 12:7,8).

Satan and his fallen angels deceive. Satan is a liar and the father of liars, according to what Jesus said. His words are as follows: "Ye are of your father the devil, and the lusts of your father ye will do. He was a murderer from the beginning, and abode not in the truth, because there is no truth in him. When he speaketh a lie, he speaketh of his own: for he is a liar, and the father of it" (John 8:44).

Satan appears as an angel of light, in his efforts to deceive, and frequently succeeds in doing so. The Word says: "And no marvel; for satan himself is transformed into an angel of light. Therefore it is no great thing if his ministers also be transformed as ministers of righteousness; whose end shall be according to their works" (2 Cor. 11:14,15).

Some teach that the fallen angels are demons, but this cannot be true. Fallen angels have bodies, but demon spirits are disembodied spirits, presumably the spirits of departed wicked people. Their bodies are in the grave, somewhere. Their souls are in hell, and their spirits remain on earth, seeking human bodies to enter and possess. A legion of them occupied one man. People who believe in reincarnation relate experiences that transpired even thousands of years ago, in a former life. That is not so amazing, as demon spirits will depart from one person at the time of death, then enter another, and they remember the past. The Bible says: "It is appointed unto men once to die, but after this the judgement" (Heb. 9:27).

The Bible says, "Hell was prepared for the devil and his angels." But, when men choose to serve and worship satan, rather than God, they become satan's kids and will suffer with him in hell and the lake of fire. Heaven is real, hell is real, and we have the power of choice, through the exercise of our own will, so we decide our eternal destiny.

What is your decision?

Peace and tranquillity prevailed in God's kingdom, in the past eternity, prior to Lucifer's rebellion. The Bible tells us: "When the morning stars sang together, and all the sons of God shouted for joy" (Job 38:7). The term "sons of God" implies both male and female, and this is true in the Old Testament as well as the New.

Lucifer and his angels were originally sons of God also, but after they sinned, they were no longer referred to as sons of God. The Bible calls them "satan's angels" and "the angels that kept not their first estate." Lucifer and his angels were guilty of willful, premeditated, determined rebellion. The Scriptures do not suggest the possibility of any time in the future eternity when they will be reinstated in God's grace and fellowship.

Satan became the god of this world, and all who choose, by an act of their own will, to worship and serve him through this present lifetime, will be cast into hell and the lake of fire with him.

When Lucifer led his angels into heaven, determined to usurp God, he and his angels were defeated and cast out. As the god of this world, he knows that his time is short.

There will be another war in heaven, between Michael and his angels, and satan and his angels, while the tribulation is in progress. At that time, satan, symbolized as a great red dragon, and the devil, will be cast out of heaven the second time. He and his fallen angels will be cast to the earth, and the Bible says; "Woe to the inhabitants of the earth."

The Bible further states: "And I heard a loud voice saying in heaven, Now is come salvation, and strength, and the kingdom of our God, and the power of His Christ: for the accuser of our brethren is cast down, which accused them before our God day and night" (Rev. 12:10).

Satan and his angels will not be free to visit heaven again, after they are cast into the earth, so his vile accusations before the throne of God will be terminated. There will be great rejoicing in heaven, but the inhabitants of the earth will suffer from satan's onslaught. The Bible tells us: "Therefore rejoice, 'YE HEAVENS' and ye that dwell in 'THEM.' Woe to the inhabitors of the earth and of the sea! For the devil is come down unto you, having great wrath, because he knoweth that he hath but a short time" (Rev. 12:12).

Sinners, who have boasted loud and long, concerning their love for the devil and allegiance to him, will suddenly discover what fools they have been. But, it will be too late for all who have wilfully hardened their hearts against God, blasphemed the Holy Spirit, worshiped the devil, and received the mark of the beast. It will be a time of unprecedented evil and suffering upon earth, as the Bible says:

> And the kings of the earth, and the great men, and the rich men, and the chief captains, and the mighty men, and every bondman, and every free man, hid themselves in the dens and in the rocks of the mountains; And said to the mountains and rocks, Fall on us, and hide us from the face of him that sitteth on the throne, and from the wrath of the Lamb: For the great day of his wrath is come; and who shall be able to stand? (Rev. 6:15-17).

Now is the day of salvation. Now is the time to repent, seek the Lord, surrender to His will, serve and honor Him until we hear Him say, "Come up higher, good and faithful servant, enter into the joys of your Lord." Tomorrow may be too late. Jesus said, "For what is a man profited, if he shall gain the whole world, and lose his own soul? Or what shall a man give in exchange for his soul?" (Matt. 16:26).

Bible prophecy is being fulfilled daily, which provides undeniable evidence of the authenticity of God's Word. The Apostle Paul spoke prophetically, of these days when he said: "Now the Spirit speaketh expressly, that in the latter times some shall depart from the faith, giving heed to seducing spirits, and doctrines of devils; Speaking lies in hypocrisy; having their conscience seared with a hot iron" (1 Tim. 4:1,2).

While millions are seeking God for increasing faith and a deepening experience, others have lost the burden for souls, become engrossed in worldly pleasures and pursuits, and have fallen into a state of lukewarmness.

Satan is determined to destroy as many gullible souls as possible, in every imaginable way, and is doing so with the cooperation of many professing Christians, who "have a form of godliness, but deny the power thereof."

The Apostle Paul was inspired to write as follows: "This know also, that in the last days perilous times shall come. For men shall be lovers of their own selves, covetous, boasters, proud, blasphemers, disobedient to parents, unthankful, unholy, without natural affection, trucebreakers, false accusers, incontinent, fierce, despisers of those that are good, Traitors, heady, highminded, lovers of pleasures more than lovers of God; Having a form of godliness, but denying the power thereof: from such turn away" (2 Tim. 3:1–5).

Those who "FALL AWAY," without returning to God in humble repentance, will no doubt be categorized with the dead branches, that Jesus refers to in John 15:5,6, that are cast into the fire and burned.

Those who persist in living in sin, after falling away from the faith, will once again establish themselves in their sinful lifestyle and renew their allegiance to satan, for the Bible says: "He that committeth sin (that is to practice sin habitually) is of the devil; for the devil sinneth from the beginning. For this purpose the Son of God was manifested, that He might destroy the works of the devil" (1 John 3:8).

Over and over and over again, we are admonished in the Word to be faithful to the end. Jesus said: "But he that shall endure unto the end, the same shall be saved" (Matt. 24:13).

The Bible also says: "Watch ye therefore, and pray always,

that ye may be accounted worthy to escape all these things that shall come to pass, and to stand before the Son of man" (Luke 21:36). If it is not seriously dangerous for a born-again Christian to fall back into sin again, why has God chosen to provide so many warning signs along this road to heaven? People cannot fall from nothing. The phrase "FALL WAY" implies departing from the faith and falling into total apostasy, which in turn implies eternal separation from the Father.

Paul warns us again when He said: "Let no man deceive you by any means: for that day shall not come, except there come a falling away first, and that man of sin be revealed, the son of perdition" (2 Thess. 2:3). The son of perdition is none other than the Antichrist.

Again he said, "Take heed, brethren, lest there be in any of you an evil heart of unbelief, in departing from the living God. But exhort one another daily, while it is called Today; lest any of you be hardened through the deceitfulness of sin. For we are made partakers of Christ, if we hold the beginning of our confidence steadfast unto the end" (Heb. 3:12–14).

We are admonished to: "Follow peace with all men, and holiness, without which no man shall see the Lord" (Heb. 12:14). If professing Christians scoff at the possibility of living a holy life, by the grace of God, and only by the grace of God is it possible, they are skating on thin ice, as the saying is, and endangering their relationship with God, whether they believe it or not.

The warning signs are not to be ignored, for He further said: "For it is impossible for those who were once enlightened, and have tasted of the heavenly gift, AND WERE MADE PARTAKERS OF THE HOLY GHOST, AND HAVE TASTED THE GOOD WORD OF GOD, AND THE POWERS OF THE WORLD TO COME, if they shall FALL AWAY, to renew them again unto repentance; seeing they crucify to themselves the Son of God afresh, and put Him to an open shame" (Heb. 6:4–6).

Some well-meaning theologians have seriously relied upon

106

their own intellectual ability in the interpretation of certain passages of Scripture, rather than trust the Holy Spirit for divine guidance. Wrong interpretations could result in dire consequences for those who get the wrong impression. Remember, God always provides the grace for those who are willing to go all of the way with Him, that He may be glorified. God is not blessed when His kids live in a state of passivity.

His blessed exhortations are to be responded to in love and sincerity, such as: "And we desire that every one of you do show the same diligence to the full assurance of hope unto the end: That ye be not slothful, but followers of them who through faith and patience inherit the promises" (Heb. 6:11,12).

By living a dedicated life to our Lord's will and service, we have nothing to lose, but everything to gain, for He said, "He that overcometh shall inherit all things; and I will be his God and he shall be My son" (Rev. 21:7). This is a good verse to memorize.

Since the fall of satan and his angels, and the subsequent Fall of man, men and nations have followed the downward course. The minority who have chosen to worship and serve the Lord have faced much opposition, have fought bravely in this spiritual conflict, and millions have died as martyrs. God has no place for cowards in His army, and He has provided a complete set of armor for our protection against satanic attacks, but as soldiers we are expected to train for the battle and to learn how to protect ourselves.

All who choose to identify themselves with satan and his evil henchmen are included in his fall, and since they have made their choice, they must also accept the consequences. The Bible provides conclusive, prophetical evidence of their destiny. Consider the horrendous, and utterly hopeless future of all who defy God, reject His salvation, and choose to live for and like the devil. God's Word says:

And the devil that deceived them was cast into the lake of fire and brimstone, where the beast and the false prophet are, and shall be tormented day and night forever and ever. And I saw a great white throne, and Him that sat on it, from whose face the earth and the heaven fled away; and there was found no place for them.

And I saw the dead, small and great, stand before God; and the books were opened: and another book was opened, which is the book of life: and the dead were judged out of those things which were written in the books, according to their works. And the sea gave up the dead which were in it; and death and hell delivered up the dead which were in them: and they were judged every man according to their works.

And death and hell were cast into the lake of fire. This is the second death. And whosoever was not found written in the book of life was cast into the lake of fire (Rev. 20:10–15).

Satan, his fallen angels, and all who have identified with them, will receive their just retribution, and God's loyal followers will never again be subjected to opposition from evil powers.

God's Guardian Angels

The Bible provides examples in which God's guardian angels fulfilled their mission, by protecting God's servants. For example, consider the three Hebrew men who were cast into Nebuchadnezzar's hot, burning furnace, because they flat refused to bow to his great image: "Then Nebuchadnezzar spake, and said, Blessed be the God of Sha'drach, Me'shach, and A-bed'-ne-go, who hath sent His 'ANGEL,' and delivered His servants that trusted in Him, and have changed the king's word, and yielded their bodies, that they might not serve or worship any god, except their own God" (Dan. 3:28).

Daniel also testified of angelic protection when he was cast into the lion's den, because of the conniving actions of his peers in government. King Darius was deceived into signing a decree into law, which was formed by Daniel's enemies because of their jealous hatred of Daniel. The king was compelled to allow Daniel to be cast into the den of ravenous lions, because of the law of the Medes and the Persians, but the king had no rest that night. Early the following morning, he went to the den of lions, and with a lamentable voice called to Daniel: "O Daniel, servant of the living God, is thy God, whom thou servest continually, able to deliver thee from the lions?

"Then said Daniel unto the king, O king, live forever. My God sent His 'ANGEL,' and hath shut the lions' mouths, that they have not hurt me: forasmuch as before Him innocency was found in me; and also before thee, O king, have I done no hurt" (Dan. 6:20–22).

When Elijah, the servant of the Lord, fled into the wilderness because of his fear of Jezebel and her evil threats, God sent a guardian angel to protect and direct the prophet. Elijah prayed for death, but God was not finished with him yet, so the angel provided food, encouragement, and direction. The record is as follows:

> But he himself went a day's journey into the wilderness, and came and sat down under a juniper tree: and he requested for himself that he might die; and said, It is enough; now, O Lord, take away my life; for I am not better than my fathers. And as he lay and slept under a juniper tree, behold, then an "ANGEL" touched him, and said unto him, Arise and eat.
>
> And he looked, and, behold, there was a cake baked on the coals, and a cruse of water at his head. And he did eat and drink, and laid him down again. And the "ANGEL" of the Lord came again the second time, and touched him, and said, Arise and eat; because the journey is too great for thee. And he arose, and did eat and drink, and went in the strength of that meat forty days and forty nights unto Horeb the mount of God (1 Kings 19:4–8).

We have the assurance of angelic protection when a proper attitude toward the Lord is maintained. He said: "The angel of the Lord encampeth round about them that fear Him, and delivereth them" (Ps.34:7). This fear does not bring torment, but it implies proper respect for God, reverence, and an earnest desire to be fully obedient to the will of our heavenly Father. In this respect, it is similar to God's promises as recorded in other scriptural references, such as: "He that dwelleth in the secret place of the most High shall abide under the shadow of the Almighty. Because thou hast made the Lord, which is my refuge, even the most High, thy habitation; There shall no evil befall thee, neither shall any plague come nigh thy dwelling. For He shall give His 'ANGELS' charge over thee, to keep thee in all thy ways" (Ps. 91:1,9–11).

What a joy and comfort it is to know that we are in the hands of God, to enjoy His peace, blessing, guidance, and strength. We have nothing to fear, or worry about, when we are trusting fully in Him.

An incident occurred in the Philippines in 1958, while we were serving as missionaries, that left us with lasting memories and deep, personal gratitude to our wonderful Lord. I had driven our 1955 Studebaker from our home in Manila to the Jones district in north central Luzon. While there I parked the car in the yard of a Christian family, and we went up river by boat to minister on the Maddela district.

While we were there, the rainy season began and flood water flowed down the river from the mountainous region. We were somewhat concerned as we had a low-water bridge to cross. It was a one-way, narrow bridge, with no railings. I had two young pastors with me.

As we approached the bridge our concern increased, for the bridge was covered with water. We paused at the edge of the wide, flooding river, trying to decide whether or not to attempt the crossing. At that point in time, a bus, well loaded with passengers, approached the river and began to cross. I noticed that the water was only about one foot deep, flowing over the bridge, so we decided to follow the bus.

We proceeded satisfactorily for the first part of the crossing, but then we noticed the depth of the water above the bridge continued to increase. Both of my passengers were praying very sincerely and even emotionally, and I joined in, as we expected to be washed off the bridge at any moment, due to the force of the rapidly flowing flood waters.

Nearing the far shore of the river, the water was splashing against the lower side of the windows on the upriver side. The motor continued to run smoothly. The bus stopped on the shore, the passengers crowded out of the bus, and they stood in amazement watching our approach. The people declared it was a miracle. I believe our guardian angel saved us. God was not yet finished with us.

The fact that Lucifer and his angels fell and forfeited their inheritance in the kingdom of God, and likewise man sinned against God and became a fallen, debased, sinful race, does not necessitate the eternal damnation of all humans.

God, in His great love, grace, mercy, and righteousness, is to be thanked, praised, and worshiped because of His Grand Redemptive Design.

Thank God for men who stand for truth and righteousness, in divine fellowship, who refuse to bow to the god of this world, and who boldly witness, admonishing intelligent human beings to receive Christ Jesus into their hearts and lives and learn to "live and walk in the Spirit." May our prayer be:

> God, give us men. A time like this demands strong minds, great hearts, true faith and ready hands; Men whom the lust of office does not kill; Men whom the spoils of office cannot buy; Men who possess opinions and a will;

Men who have honor, men who will not lie; Men who can stand before a demagogue, And damn his treacherous flatteries without winking; Tall men, sun-crowned, who live above the fog, In public duty and in private thinking; For while the rabble with their thumb-worn creeds, Their large professions and their little deeds; Mingle in selfish strife—lo, freedom weeps, Wrong rules the land, and waiting justice sleeps.

God, give us men; Men who serve not for selfish booty, But real men, courageous, who flinch not at duty; Men of dependable character; men of sterling worth; Then wrongs will be redressed, and right will rule on earth. God, GIVE US MEN. (Selected)

Since the Fall of man, only one TRUE MAN has walked upon this planet, the Man Christ Jesus. But, millions have patterned their lives after Him, and by His grace are becoming more like Him, and "when we see Him, we shall be like Him."

God's Warrior Angels

God has armies of loyal, ANGELIC WARRIORS, in His vast, endless, universal, governmental kingdom, and He wisely designates their duties. Jesus said to Peter: "Put up again thy sword into his place: for all that take the sword shall perish with the sword.

"Thinkest thou that I cannot pray to My Father, and He shall presently give me more than twelve legions of angels? But how then shall the scriptures be fulfilled, that thus it must be?" (Matt. 26:52–54).

Judas, the traitor, had led a multitude to arrest Jesus. Peter had a sword and proceeded to use it by cutting off the right ear of Malchus, a servant of the high priest. Can you visualize Malchus, dancing around, with his right hand clasped tightly over the bleeding stub of his ear, screaming threatenings of dire consequences against Peter? Jesus quickly stooped over, picked up the bloody ear, clamped it back to the side of Malchus' head, and healed it, saying, "Now where is your evidence?" John tells us the servant's name was Malchus (John 18:10).

Jesus could have called more than twelve legions of angels to rescue Him and destroy His enemies, but He chose to fulfill the divine mandate, take His place on a cruel cross, and become our Redeemer. A legion, in the Roman army, consisted of 3,000 to 6,000 foot soldiers, plus 500 to 700 cavalry. We could safely estimate that Jesus could have called at least 60,000 angels to His rescue, but had He done so, the plan of redemption would have been defeated, and the entire human race would have been lost. So, He took your place and mine, and poured forth His precious life's blood, to redeem us from sin and eternal hell. Have you thanked HIM?

The Bible provides many references of activities on the part of God's Warrior Angels. We invite your attention to a few.

Joshua was unable to distinguish an angel from a human being, but when he challenged him, the angel introduced himself. The record states: "And it came to pass, when Joshua was by Jericho, that he lifted up his eyes and looked, and, behold, there stood a man over against him with his sword drawn in his hand: and Joshua went to him, and said unto him, Art thou for us, or for our adversaries?

"And he said, Nay; but as the captain of the host of the Lord am I now come. And Joshua fell on his face to the earth, and did worship, and said unto him, What saith my lord unto his servant? (Joshua 5:13,14).

God's warrior angels are watching over the servants of the Lord and assisting in warfare against the enemies of the Lord and His people. God gave Joshua and the children of Israel a decisive victory over the city and inhabitants of Jericho. Many of God's servants would be easily defeated and destroyed were it not for our warrior angels who fight for us.

We read of a state of war existing between the king of Israel and the king of Syria and their armies. In this major conflict, the king of Syria was greatly disturbed because of ambushes that were the cause of his defeat, on several occasions. Elisha, the man of God, revealed the battle plans of the king of Syria, to the king of Israel, and thus enabled him to gain an advantage. The Bible says, "Therefore the heart of the king of Syria was sore troubled for this thing: and he called his servants, and said unto them, Will you not show me which of us is for the king of Israel?

"And one of his servants said, None, my lord, O king: but Elisha,the prophet that is in Israel, telleth the king of Israel the words that thou speakest in thy bedchamber" (2 Kings 6:11,12).

The king of Syria then sent his servants to seek for Elisha and they informed him that the prophet was in Dothan. An interesting event then occurred.

> So the king of Syria sent forth horses, and chariots, with a great host, by night, surrounding the city, and planning to capture Elisha. Elisha's servant rising early in the morning was fearful when he saw the city surrounded by the Syrian army, so he said: "Alas, my master! How shall we do?" Elisha said, "Fear not; for they that be with us are more than they that be with them." Elisha then prayed that the Lord would open the eyes of his servant, and the Lord did so (2 Kings 6:15–17).

The young man was utterly astounded when his spiritual vision was quickened, and he saw the mountain was full of horses and chariots round about Elisha. When our spiritual eyes are opened, and our spiritual conception active, our fear departs and our faith takes over.

The true nature of Elisha took control of the situation when he prayed for the Lord to smite the Syrian army with blindness. The Lord did so and Elisha led the blind army to Samaria. The king of Israel asked: "Shall I smite them?" Elisha reasoned with the king and advised him to feed them. When they had finished their meal, the king of Israel sent them away, and the war was discontinued for a time.

The major population of planet earth is suffering from spiritual blindness, being deceived by the devil and his emissaries. When they are willing to acknowledge their pitiful condition, open their minds and hearts to TRUTH, they will experience spiritual life and vision and move in fellowship with the Lord and His redeemed people. Why grope in darkness and ignorance when Jesus is the WAY, the TRUTH, and the LIFE? He alone is the LIGHT of the world, and in HIM is no darkness. The Bible says: "In HIM was LIFE; and the life was the light of men. And the light shineth in darkness; And the darkness comprehended it not" (John 1:4,5).

If God had provided no Bible, no Redeemer, and no source of

knowledge concerning man's origin, composition, purpose and destiny, man would have had no hope for better things to come. But since HE has provided the Bible, which is man's only true source of knowledge, also a Redeemer, plus power to live a victorious Christian life, man is without excuse. If he chooses, by an act of his own will, to serve and worship satan rather than God, he will suffer the consequences of his fatal decision eternally.

"For the invisible things of him from the creation of the world are clearly seen, being understood by the things which are made, even His eternal power and Godhead; so that they are without excuse: Because that, when they knew God, they glorified Him not as God, neither were thankful; but became vain in their imaginations, and their foolish heart was darkened. Professing themselves to be wise, they became fools" (Rom. 1:20–22).

In humble surrender to the will of God, we have the assurance of angelic assistance, in all battles against satanic powers. When King Hezekiah prayed before the Lord, at a time when Sennacherib, pagan king of Assyria, and his army surrounded Jerusalem, God sent His angel warrior to Israel's assistance. As the Bible record states: "And it came to pass that night, that the angel of the Lord went out, and smote in the camp of the Assyrians 185,000, and when they arose in the morning, behold, they were all dead corpses. So Sennacherib king of Assyria departed, and went and returned, and dwelt at Nineveh" (2 Kings 19:35,36).

Those who loudly boast of what they have done, and intend to do, in wilfully opposing God and His people, are providing a gallows on which to hang themselves.

Another war is described in Revelation, when God's loyal angels will defeat the devil and his angels the second time. The Bible says:

And there was war in heaven: Michael and his angels fought against the dragon; and the dragon fought and his angels, and prevailed not; neither was their place found any more in heaven. And the great dragon was cast out, that old serpent, called the devil, and satan, which deceiveth the whole world: he was cast out into the earth, and his angels were cast out with him.

And I heard a loud voice saying in heaven, "Now is come salvation, and strength, and the kingdom of our God, and the power of His CHRIST: for the accuser of our brethren is cast down, which accused them before our God day and night" (Rev. 12:7–10).

Some have erroneously applied this prophecy to the war fought between angels in the past eternity, when Lucifer ambitiously determined to enlarge his kingdom, by usurping God Himself (Isa. 14:12–15).

The war described in Revelation 12:7–17, along with God's dealings with Israel, pertains to the future, and will be fulfilled during the seven year period of tribulation. A careful and prayerful analysis of this prophecy makes this very clear.

Michael, the archangel, and his loyal angelic warriors, will win a decisive victory over the devil and his fallen angels.

That segment of the nation of Israel, that births the manchild (144,000), Jews out of Israel, will flee into a wilderness in Israel, where they will be protected for the last three and one half years, of the seven-year period. Antichrist and his evil forces will not be able to apprehend them, because God has promised to protect them. The spiritual revival will continue in Israel, and their seven-point spiritual restoration will be accomplished, according to Daniel 9:24–26.

To be identified with God and His forces is to be on the winning side.

God's Angel Messengers

God's angel messengers delivered divine knowledge, hope, and positive assurance of victory, on various occasions, as recorded in the Word.

For example: Abraham took Hagar, Sarah's maid, as a second wife, acting on Sarah's advice. When Hagar conceived, she demonstrated a critical spirit toward Sarah, so Sarah retaliated, and Hagar fled into the wilderness, where one of God's angelic messengers met her.

And he said, Hagar, Sarai's maid, where did you come from and where are you going? And she said, I flee from the face of my mistress Sa'rai. And the angel said unto her, Return to your mistress and submit yourself to her. And the angel of the Lord said unto her, Behold, you are with child, and shall give birth to a son, and shall call his name Ishmael; because the Lord has seen your affliction. And he shall be a wild man; his hand will be against every man, and every man's hand against him; and he shall dwell in the presence of all his brethren (Gen. 16:8–12. Modern English).

So Hagar returned and was submissive to Sarah. In due time she delivered a son: and Abraham called his son's name, Ishmael.

When Abraham was ninety-nine years of age, the Lord promised him a son by his wife Sarah, as her name was changed at that time, from Sarai to Sarah. Sarah was ninety years of age and had been barren all of the years of her married life.

Abraham made a great feast the day Isaac was weaned, and Ishmael, past thirteen years of age, mocked. The tension reached a climax between Sarah and Hagar, so Sarah demanded that Hagar and Ishmael be sent away. The Lord advised Abraham likewise.

The angel of the Lord appeared to them in the wilderness, the second time, when they were destitute, and delivered God's message (Gen. 21:12–21).

The event is recorded as follows: "And Abraham rose up early in the morning, and took bread, and a bottle of water, and gave it to Hagar, putting it on her shoulder, and the child, and sent her away; and she departed, and wandered in the wilderness of Be'er-she'ba. And the water was spent in the bottle, and she cast the child under one of the shrubs. And she went, and sat her down over against him a good way off, as it were a bowshot: for she said, Let me not see the death of the child. And she sat over against him, and lifted up her voice and wept" (Gen. 21:14–16).

There are several valuable lessons to be learned from this incident. When God revealed his will to Abraham, there was no hesitation. Abraham arose early in the morning and proceeded to act upon the Lord's instructions. It was a painful experience because he loved Ishmael, his first son, also. When we learn to put God first in our lives, and become familiar with His Word, recognizing His voice when He speaks to our hearts, He directs us always in the right way.

When the angel communicated with Hagar in the wilderness the first time, he promised that her son would become prominent. But when her food and water supply was exhausted, faith took wings, flew away, and left doubt and fear in control. She expected death for herself and Ishmael. How easy it is to forget the promises of God in the midst of trials.

Again, the angel appeared to her and her eyes were opened so she could see the well of water. God was with the lad, he grew, became a successful hunter and dwelt in the wilderness of Paran. His mother took him a wife out of the land of Egypt. God fulfilled the promise He had made to Abraham concerning Isaac: "And as for Ishmael, I have heard thee: Behold I have blessed him, and will make him fruitful, and will multiply him exceedingly; twelve princes shall he beget, and I will make him a great nation" (Gen. 17:20).

The twelve princes became twelve Arab nations, and all of their descendants claim Abraham as their father, and rightly so.

Before the people had the Bible to serve as a guide, God frequently sent His angel messengers to convey His will and Word to the people. The Holy Spirit also speaks to our hearts and gives direction, as in the life of Paul the Apostle. The record states: "Now when they had gone throughout Phrygia and the region of Galatia, and were forbidden of the Holy Ghost to preach the word in Asia, after they were come to Mysia, they assayed to go into Bithynia: but the Spirit suffered them not" (Acts 16:6,7).

The Bible provides other very interesting and even exciting incidents in which angelic messengers were sent to reveal God's plan. Zechariah, while in the process of fulfilling his priestly office, received an exciting message when an angel messenger appeared to him according to the Word: "And there appeared unto him an angel of the Lord standing on the right side of the altar of incense. And when Zechariah saw him, he was troubled, and fear fell upon him. But the angel said unto him, Fear not, Zechariah: for thy prayer is heard; and thy wife Elizabeth shall bear thee a son, and thou shalt call his name John" (Luke 1:11–13).

God sent Gabriel, one of the leading angels, to apprise Mary of the great honor to be granted unto her. He said: "Fear not, Mary: for thou hast found favor with God. And, behold, thou shalt conceive in thy womb, and bring forth a son, and shalt call His name JESUS" (Luke 1:30,31).

When Joseph learned that Mary was with child, he assumed that she was guilty of fornication, so he planned to cancel the marriage: "But while he thought on these things, behold, the angel of the Lord appeared unto him in a dream, saying, Joseph, thou son of David, fear not to take unto thee Mary thy wife: for that which is conceived in her is of the Holy Ghost. And she shall bring forth a son, and thou shalt call his name JESUS: for He shall save His people from their sins" (Matt. 1:20,21).

The Bible relates numerous other incidents of activities on the part of God's angel messengers, but for this study, one more familiar event will suffice. The Apostle Paul had been arrested, had appealed to Caesar, and was en route to Rome by ship.

Due to stormy seas, he advised a postponement of their voyage in the following words: "Sirs, I perceive that this voyage will be with hurt and much damage, not only of the lading and ship, but also of our lives" (Acts 27:10).

However, the captain of the ship, and also the owner, rejected Paul's warning, and they continued on their voyage.

Rather than diminishing, the wind increased in velocity and their ship was tossed about in the tempestuous storm. They lightened the ship, but to no avail. Paul then delivered God's message and assured them that all 276 passengers would be spared, when he said: "Men, you should have listened to me, and not have sailed from Crete and incurred this disaster and loss. And now I urge you to take heart, for there will be no loss of life among you, but only the ship. For there stood by me this night an angel of God to whom I belong and whom I serve, saying, 'Do not be afraid, Paul; you must be brought before Caesar; and indeed God has granted you all those who sail with you.' Therefore take heart, men, for I believe God that it will be just as it was told me" (Acts 27:21–25 NKJV).

Many years ago a yacht was cruising among the isles of Scotland, when a strong gale blew up. The skipper aimed for a harbor some distance away, and as they sailed, they were overtaken by darkness. Finally, after a hazardous voyage, they swung into the safe harbour. The following morning the owner went on deck, surveyed the scene, noting the narrow approach to the harbour, with jagged rocks jutting out on both sides, and he was amazed that they had avoided shipwreck.

Do Angels Reproduce?

Theologians, generally, have ministered under the assumption that angels do not reproduce. Some teach that all angels, in their different orders, are male, and that God created billions of them individually.

Others teach that all angels are sexless. Students in Bible College brought these questions to my attention years ago, when I had no satisfactory Bible answers to give them. Their questions aroused my own curiosity and I began a systematic, concentrated study of the Scriptures, concerning angels.

After some years of study on the subject, as time permitted from time to time, I eventually arrived at certain conclusions and firm convictions, supported both by the Scriptures and logic. In questioning the reasons for assuming certain positions that we consider to be misinterpretations of the Bible, the brethren habitually base their reply on the words of Jesus, in reply to the unbelieving Sadducees, who interrogated Jesus concerning the woman who had seven husbands.

They did not believe in angels, nor did they believe in the resurrection, but they were merely interested in learning what Jesus would say. He never, at any time, revealed the mysteries of the kingdom of heaven to unbelievers.

Jesus merely replied by saying: "You are mistaken, not knowing the Scriptures nor the power of God. For in the resurrection they neither marry nor are given in marriage, but are like the angels of God in heaven" (Matt. 22:29,30).

He could have explained that there would be no marriages in

heaven such as they were familiar with on earth, in this present life. He could have explained that God's mating system in the future life would be similar to what it was in the past eternity. He said we would be like the angels.

Furthermore, Jesus did not say the angels are all male, or all sexless, nor did He say the redeemed, immortal saints will be sexless, nor did He say there would be no babies born in the future life. God has chosen to give us glimpses into the future eternity, and the picture is beautiful and perfect.

As has been stated previously, in this series of biblical studies, the purpose of redemption is to fully restore man to what he was prior to the Fall, and restore to him every good thing God provided for him in the Garden of Eden. Otherwise, we would have only a partial redemption. We must further understand that all of the laws instituted after man's Fall are temporary, including all laws of marriage, in their many different forms and stages, down through the centuries. When God's redeemed, immortal children are ushered out onto the New Earth, and into the New Heavens, all of these temporary laws will be abolished. Therefore, He is telling us that all of the legality of marriage, as the laws have existed in this life, will be abolished.

In along with future eternity, the redeemed saints, God's loyal angels, will be subject to HIS higher laws, namely: "For the law of the Spirit of life in Christ Jesus has made me free from the law of sin and death.

"For what the law could not do in that it was weak through the flesh, God did by sending His own Son in the likeness of sinful flesh, on account of sin. He condemned sin in the flesh, that the RIGHTEOUS requirement of the law might be fulfilled in us, who do not walk according to the flesh but according to the Spirit" (Rom. 8:2–4. NKJV).

Since there will be no sin, sickness, or death, in God's glorious, future kingdom, all temporary laws, affecting man's carnality, in his mortal state, will be abolished. God's higher, eternal, spiritual laws, will prevail. Can you believe it?

There is scriptural evidence indicating that angels are both male and female, and if so, why would they not be productive? If angels do not reproduce, according to their own kind, and according to God's Divine pattern in creation, they are the only source of life in God's vast universal system that does not do so.

God instituted laws, at the very beginning of His creation, according to all available biblical information, requiring that every form of life, from the flea to the elephant, would reproduce according to its own kind. There have been degrees of evolution within the individual species, but never a cross between major species, producing offspring that are capable of reproducing. Freaks of nature do not reproduce according to their own kind.

May I ask a question? If angels do not reproduce, according to their own kind, and gradually within the eternal plan of God, then why not? Since God has created billions of galaxies, according to our leading astronomers who tell us there are indeed billions of galaxies in outer space, is it impossible to believe that angels will continue to reproduce eternally, along with the immortal children of God? God does all things well.

If God created billions of angels, individually, running them off on a special type of assembly line, as some suppose, why did he not create billions of humans also? Both angels and humans are spirit beings.

Many very special surprises will confront us when we arrive in heaven and also on the New Earth. The reality will be many times greater than our most vivid imagination.

The Bible provides various references concerning the "SONS OF GOD," in the Old Testament as well as the New. In both the Hebrew and the Greek, the term implies both male and female. Notice the following references.

"When the morning stars sang together, and all the sons of

God shouted for joy?" The Lord was talking to Job at the time, reminding him of events that had transpired in the past eternity.

Obviously, there was a time of special rejoicing among the angelic sons of God, when only harmony reigned supremely, in God's kingdom. The word "sons" is translated from the Hebrew word "BEN" pronounced "BANE," according to *Strong's Exhaustive Concordance,* which is recognized as one of the most reliable of the concordances. The word "BEN" has different definitions, including son, one born, child, daughter, colt, and others. We may therefore successfully conclude that daughters were included with the sons of God referred to (Gen. 6:2), and other references to the "SONS OF GOD."

This is also true in the New Testament. Our English word "sons," as translated from the Greek word "*tek'-non*" is translated into our words "child, daughter, son." The phrase "SONS OF GOD" includes both sons and daughters. For example: "But as many as received Him, to them gave He power to become the sons of God, even to them that believe on His Name" (John 1:12).

The same Greek word is used in the following verses, indicating that both sons and daughters are included in the reference, as follows:

"Behold, what manner of love the Father hath bestowed on us, that we should be called the SONS OF GOD: therefore the world knoweth us not, because it knew Him not.

"Beloved, now are we the SONS OF GOD, and it doth not yet appear what we shall be: but we know that, when He shall appear, we shall be like Him; for we shall see Him as He is" (1 John 3:1,2).

Zechariah the prophet had a vision of two female angels and described what he saw. He said: "Then I raised my eyes and looked. And there were two women, coming with the wind in their wings; for they had wings like the wings of a stork, and they lifted up the basket between earth and heaven.

"So I said to the angel who talked with me, 'Where are they carrying the basket?' And he said to me, 'To build a house for it in the land of Shinar; when it is ready, the basket will be set there on its base' " (Zech. 5:9,10. NKJV).

There is no indication in the context that the above verses are to be interpreted symbolically. No commentary that I have read provides an adequate interpretation of the event. When any portion of Scripture is to be interpreted symbolically or spiritually, there will be an indication either in the context or in related passages. When no such indication is evident, we must interpret them literally. The prophet saw two women with wings. If they were not female angels, who were they?

God has some wonderful Christian women who have fully dedicated their lives to His service, and they demonstrate angelic characteristics, but they do not have wings.

Some years ago when I began teaching the existence of female angels, some ridiculed the idea; others were open-minded, sincere, and open-hearted to the Word. There were still others who openly agreed with the teaching. One lady said, "I have believed in female angels for years, because when my dear Christian mother departed this life, I saw a female angel standing at the foot of her bed. Who do you think is caring for the multiplied millions of babies who have been aborted? They are cruelly murdered here on earth, and God's angels accompany them to heaven, where they are cared for."

Another lady informed her pastor, who is a personal friend of mine, that two angels had appeared to her in a time of loneliness, after the passing of her husband. She said that one of them was a male and the other one a female.

God has not chosen to give us a detailed account of heaven's present population, or the inhabitants of perhaps thousands of planets in outer space, because detailed accounts of conditions we consider to be mysterious are not vital to our salvation. But He has given us a degree of revelation in the Bible, and we need to maintain a teachable attitude at all times, or the Holy Spirit cannot lead us into deeper areas of truth.

Concerning young children, Jesus said: "Take heed that ye despise not one of these little ones; for I say unto you, That in heaven their angels do always behold the face of My Father which is in heaven" (Matt. 18:10).

When the Apostle Paul was caught up to paradise, he had an unusual experience. He said: "I knew a man in Christ above fourteen years ago, (whether in the body, I cannot tell; or whether out of the body, I cannot tell: God knoweth;) such an one caught up to the third heaven. And I knew such a man, (whether in the body, or out of the body, I cannot tell: God knoweth;)

"How that he was caught up into paradise, and heard unspeakable words, which it is not lawful for a man to utter. Of such an one will I glory: yet of myself I will not glory, but in mine infirmities" (2 Cor. 12:2–5).

Apparently Paul saw some things, and heard some things, that he was not permitted to speak of when he returned to earth. In checking the dates, it seems that his visit to heaven coincided with the stoning he received at Lystra, when his body was taken out of the city and he was left for dead (Acts 14:19,20).

One humble servant of the Lord declared: "What God calls a man to do, he will carry through. I would undertake to govern half a dozen worlds if God called me to do it; but if He did not call me to do it, I would not undertake to govern half a dozen sheep" (Selected).

Jesus said: "But the Comforter, which is the Holy Ghost, whom the Father will send in my name, He shall teach you all things, and bring all things to your remembrance, whatsoever I have said unto you" (John 14:26).

Many conclusions, relative to the will of God for our lives, and understanding of His Word, are arrived at through the exercise of our intellectual ability. Quite frequently these conclusions do not coincide with the Word of God. It is difficult to unlearn opinions and even convictions, in certain areas, and accept new and more scriptural interpretations. We learn from listening to others who are on the right biblical track, and trusting the Holy Spirit for divine guidance.

When God gives us the true witness of the Spirit, pertaining to any portion of truth, we feel comfortable with it and the conviction grows, until we fully believe what He tells us, and we desire to share it with others. Truth invariably increases our faith and enables us to become more productive in our Master's service.

Jesus said, "You shall know the truth and the truth shall make you free." He also said, "If you hunger and thirst after righteousness you shall be filled."

It is time, brethren, to seek God earnestly for everything He desires for us to have.

Angels in Revelation

The Book of Revelation, not "Revelations," as some refer to it, is the Revelation of Jesus Christ, as the record declares: "The Revelation of Jesus Christ, which God gave unto Him, to show unto His servants things which must shortly come to pass; and He sent and signified it by His angel unto His servant John: Who bare record of the Word of God, and of the testimony of Jesus Christ, and of all things that he saw" (Rev. 1:1,2).

Some Christians become so involved in reading about the beasts and the plagues, recorded in this book, that they fail to recognize and appreciate the true message that our Lord desires to impart.

In this study we are considering the activities of God's loyal angels during the tribulation period, as revealed in the Book of Revelation.

The Greek word "ANG'-EL-OS," from which our word "angel" is derived, also means messenger, and could apply to the pastor messengers to the churches. Each of the seven churches received special messages from the Lord and were to be delivered to the churches through the angel messengers, or pastors, as the Lord directed. These seven messages were delivered to seven leading churches in western Asia Minor, in the early days of the Church Age. They also have a prophetical significance applicable to every period of the Church Age and are being fulfilled in our day.

Pastors of local churches in our day will be held accountable for their ministry, and should they fail to deliver God's message, in love and under the direction and anointing of the Holy Spirit, they will suffer the consequences eternally.

God's rewards, for faithfulness in His service, will be indescribable. Why not be determined to go all of the way with Him and for Him?

Man's total fellowship with his Creator is regulated by the degree of obedience that he maintains. It is not for us to decide what we will do, within ourselves, but to learn to rely upon our Father's will. To know His will and do it are two separate entities. Some say, "Oh, yes, I desire to know the will of God," but, when it is revealed, they hesitate, in a spirit of uncertainty. The real joy and happiness is experienced by those who have learned to recognize the will of God, and then appropriate His power to do it.

God does not reveal His secrets, or deeper portions of truth, to spiritual babies, because they are not capable of receiving them. As we move from spiritual infancy toward maturity, step by step, He directs His progressive servants into increasing revelation and spiritual illumination. Our strong desire for increasing knowledge, along with a sincere spirit of humility, determines the rate of growth. As the Bible tells us:

"Surely the Lord God will do nothing, but He revealeth His secret unto His servants the prophets" (Amos 3:7). This is also confirmed in Proverbs 3:32, where the Bible says: "For the froward is abomination to the Lord: but His secret is with the righteous."

Shall we therefore permit the Holy Spirit to control and regulate our thought processes, as we proceed with an outline study of God's Angels in Revelation?

In chapter five of Revelation, we read of the Lamb who was slain, to redeem us to God, but He does not return to the earth as a Lamb, but as the conquering Lion of the tribe of Judah. He, the Lord Jesus Christ, is the only one worthy enough to take the scroll from the Father's right hand and break the seals thereof.

Much excitement will prevail in heaven as the Lord Jesus

Christ prepares to break the seals on the scroll. The Apostle John reported what he saw, and recorded it as follows:

> Then I looked, and I heard the voice of many angels around the throne, the living creatures, and the elders; and the number of them was ten thousand times ten thousand, and thousands of thousands, saying with a loud voice:
> "Worthy is the Lamb who was slain To receive power and riches, and wisdom, And strength and honor and glory and blessing!" (Rev. 5:11,12).

As the Lord Jesus proceeded to break the seals on the scroll, John described what he saw. He beheld four horsemen. As the first four seals were broken: the first horse was white, symbolizing peace; the second horse was red, symbolizing war; the third horse is black, symbolizing famine; and the fourth horse is pale, symbolizing death.

The rider of these four horses is one and the same, none other than the Antichrist, representing four aspects of his dictatorial reign on earth. His reign will be suddenly terminated when Christ returns to earth, with the armies from heaven, and will utterly defeat Antichrist and his army. Notice what the prophecy tells us:

> Now I saw heaven opened, and behold, a white horse. And He who sat on him was called faithful and True, and in righteousness He judges and makes war.
> He was clothed with a robe dipped in blood, and His name is called THE WORD OF GOD. And the armies in heaven, clothed in fine linen, white and clean, followed Him on white horses.
> Then the beast (anti-Christ) was captured, and with him the false prophet who worked signs in his presence, by which he deceived those who received the mark of the beast and those who worshiped his image.
> These two were cast alive into the lake of fire burning with brimstone. And the rest were killed with the sword which pro-

ceeded from the mouth of Him (His commands, as King of kings and Lord of lords) who sat on the horse. And all the birds were filled with their flesh (Rev. 19:11, 13,14, 20,21; NKJV).

Satan is very active in our day, working his will through all of his henchmen, by captivating the attention of evil-minded humans, along with the fallen angels and myriads of demonic spirits, but his time is short. The prophecy reveals his utter defeat, in the following words:

"And I saw an angel come down from heaven, having the key to the bottomless pit and a great chain in his hand. And he laid hold on the dragon, that old serpent, which is the devil, and satan, and bound him a thousand years, And cast him into the bottomless pit, and shut him up, and set a seal upon him, that he should deceive the nations no more, till the thousand years should be fulfilled: and after that he must be loosed a little season (Rev. 20:1–3).

God's seven-point restoration prophecy for Israel, as revealed in Daniel 9:24–27, is to be fulfilled when the two prophets, undoubtedly Moses and Elijah, will return to Israel and conduct special prophecy teaching meetings in Israel, which will result in their acceptance of Jesus Christ as their Messiah and Savior. God sent an angel to seal the 144,000 converted Jews, who will represent the first fruits of the restored nation of Israel, as the prophecy states:

And I saw another angel ascending from the east, having the seal of the living God: and he cried with a loud voice to the four angels, to whom it was given to hurt the earth and the sea, Saying, Hurt not the earth, neither the sea, nor the trees, till we have sealed the servants of our God in their foreheads.

And I heard the number of them which were sealed: and there were sealed an hundred and forty and four thousand from the tribes of the children of Israel (Rev. 7:2–4).

When the Lord broke the seventh seal, John saw seven angels, and to them were given seven trumpets. John was impressed by the fact that when the seal was broken, there was silence in heaven for about half an hour. Some wit said, "There will surely not be any women in heaven, because they could not keep quiet for half an hour." Of course, the women say, "How about you men?" It is possible that most of us talk too much, at times.

We are providing only a brief outline of these events, which will occur on earth, at the sounding of the seven trumpet judgments. These judgments will be poured out upon earth during the last three and one half years, of the seven-year period, which is referred to as "GREAT TRIBULATION."

1. **THE FIRST TRUMPET JUDGMENT**: Hail and fire mingled with blood will be cast upon earth. As a result a third part of the trees and all green grass will be burnt up.
2. **THE SECOND TRUMPET JUDGMENT**: A great mountain burning with fire will be cast into the sea. A third part of sea life will die and a third of the ships will be destroyed.
3. **THE THIRD TRUMPET JUDGMENT**: A great star will fall to earth and affect the rivers and fountains of waters, causing them to become contaminated and many will die.
4. **THE FOURTH TRUMPET JUDGMENT**: A third part of the sun will be smitten, and also a third part of the moon and the stars, so the third part of the day, and of the night, will be darkened.

   The scriptural record of the four Trumpet Judgments are recorded in the Book of Revelation, chapter eight, verses 7–12. The last three are recorded as follows:
5. **THE FIFTH TRUMPET JUDGMENT**: John saw a star fall from heaven, with the key of the bottomless pit, and he opened the pit, out of which came a smoke and

from the smoke a swarm of large, locustlike creatures, possessing power to torment evil men for a period of five months. Prior to the sounding of the last three trumpet judgments, John saw an angel flying through the midst of heaven, saying with a loud voice, WOE, WOE, WOE, to the inhabitants of the earth (Rev. 8:13).

The last three trumpet judgments fulfill the woes that are announced by the flying angel. John describes the locustlike creatures in Revelation 9:7–12.

6. **THE SECOND WOE AND SIXTH TRUMPET JUDGMENT**: The sixth angel sounded, four angels were loosed from their imprisonment in the Euphrates River, which were prepared for an hour, a day, and a month, and a year, to slay a third part of men. They led an army consisting of 200 million. John describes them in Revelation 9:16–21.

7. **THE THIRD WOE AND SEVENTH TRUMPET JUDGMENT**: In the days when the seventh angel begins to sound, the mystery of God shall be finished (Rev. 10:7).

From that point a succession of significant events will transpire, as prophesied (Rev. 10:8–11; 11:1–14.) As the seventh angel completed his blast on his trumpet judgment, the Bible says: "There were great voices in heaven, saying, the kingdoms of this world are become the kingdoms of our Lord, and of His Christ; and He shall reign forever and ever. And the nations were angry, and thy wrath is come, and the time of the dead, that they should be judged, and that thou shouldest give reward unto thy servants the prophets, and to the saints, and them that fear Thy name, small and great; and shouldest destroy them which destroy the earth" (Rev. 11:15, and 18).

We are living in the days the Apostle Paul referred to when he prophesied of increasing, prevalent evils on earth. Fifty years ago we could not have imagined the downward trend of ungodly, immoral, blasphemous, murdering, God-hating, Holy Spirit blaspheming humans, such as we see today. Because God does not actively and instantly destroy the wicked population, they think they are getting by, but He is patiently waiting until their cup of iniquity is filled to the brim. He does not wish to destroy the righteous with the wicked.

Then too, in HIS great love, compassion, mercy, grace, and patience, He is extending His day of mercy to allow all who so desire to receive Christ our Lord as Savior. In His own time, and in full accordance with His prophecies, judgment will come, quickly and certainly.

Yes, Paul's prophetic words are being fulfilled, when he said, "But evil men and seducers shall wax worse and worse, deceiving, and being deceived" (2 Tim. 3:13).

The hearts of many sinners are so hardened in sin and unbelief that even the judgments of God will not bring them to repentance. They have rejected God, sold out to the devil, seared their consciences, blasphemed the Holy Spirit, until they are totally possessed by evil powers. The Bible says: "Neither repented they of their murders, nor of their sorceries, nor of their fornication, nor of their thefts" (Rev. 9:21). In their devilish state of rebellion against God, His people, and His will, they will curse God and hope to die, but when hell receives them into its eternal torment, their doom is sealed.

God, our heavenly Father, has reached the total extreme, in His efforts to save this fallen, debased human race. But in spite of everything He has done, and provided, those who wilfully choose to rebel against HIM will suffer the consequences of their own satanically inspired choice. How about you?

John had been banished to the barren Island of Patmos, in the Mediterranean Sea, and while there was privileged to witness the great events that are recorded in the Book of Revelation. God did not wish for His loyal servants to live in ignorance concerning age end events.

In this study we are not going into detail relative to all angelic activities, as recorded in this book, but are dealing, primarily, with those that we consider to be most important, as they relate to the judgments of God.

"We do not sail to glory in the salt sea of our own tears, but in the red sea of our Redeemer's blood. We owe the life of our souls to the death of our Savior. It was His going into the furnace which keeps us from the flames. Man lives by death; his natural life is preserved by the death of the creature, and his spiritual life by the death of the Redeemer" (Secker).

John tells us: "And I saw another sign in heaven, great and marvelous, seven angels having the seven last plagues; for in them is filled up the wrath of God" (Rev. 15:1).

God is primarily a God of love, but when men wilfully reject His love, and go their own rebellious way, the time comes when He demonstrates His anger, and very much to the detriment of the devil, the Antichrist, the false prophet, the fallen angels, and evil humans. The greatest sin anyone can possibly commit is the wilful rejection of the Son of God, and His supreme sacrifice.

The Word tells us:

Because I have called, and ye refused; I have stretched out my hand, and no man regarded; But ye have set at nought all My counsel, and would none of My reproof: I also will laugh at your calamity; I will mock when your fear cometh; When your fear cometh as desolation, and your destruction cometh as a whirlwind; when distress and anguish cometh upon you.

THEN shall they call upon me, but I will not answer; they shall seek me early, but they shall not find me: For that they hated knowledge, and did not choose the fear of the Lord: They would none of my counsel: they despised all my reproof. Therefore shall they eat of the fruit of their own way, and be filled with their own devices.

But whoso hearkeneth unto me shall dwell safely, and shall be quiet from fear of evil (Prov. 1:24–31, 33).

John said: "Then one of the four living creatures gave to the seven angels seven golden bowls full of the wrath of God who lives forever and ever. The temple was filled with smoke from the glory of God and from His power, and no one was able to enter the temple till the seven plagues of the seven angels were completed" (Rev. 15:7,8 NKJV).

Again, we are giving only a brief outline of these seven plagues, as poured out upon the earth by the seven angels.

PLAGUE NUMBER ONE: A foul and loathsome sore came upon the men who had the mark of the beast and worshiped his image.

PLAGUE NUMBER TWO: The second angel emptied his bowl upon the sea, and it became like the blood of a dead man, and all sea life died.

PLAGUE NUMBER THREE: The third angel poured out his bowl on the rivers and springs of water, and they became blood. Do you take time each day to thank God for the pure water we are privileged to drink?

PLAGUE NUMBER FOUR: The fourth angel emptied his bowl upon the sun, and the heat of the sun will be greatly intensified, and earth's inhabitants will suffer much from the extreme heat.

PLAGUE NUMBER FIVE: The fifth angel poured out his bowl on the Antichrist's headquarters and his kingdom was darkened and the inhabitants experienced extreme pain.

PLAGUE NUMBER SIX: The sixth angel poured out his vial, or bowl, upon the great river Euphrates, and the river dried up, to prepare the way for the kings of the East. John saw three unclean spirits, like frogs, come out of the mouths of the devil, the Antichrist, and the false prophet, and go forth to gather together the armies of the earth for the battle of Armageddon. This suggests that the armies of the world will be divided into three divisions for the great age-end battle.

PLAGUE NUMBER SEVEN: The seventh angel poured out his vial into the air, which resulted in thunderings, lightnings, and a great earthquake, the greatest earthquake that had ever occurred since the creation of man. Cities will be utterly destroyed, islands will disappear into the sea, mountains will be flattened, great hailstones weighing about 100 pounds will bring death and destruction (Rev. 16:1–21).

NOTE: The description of the seven plagues is not copied word for word from the Bible, but given in my own words in part.

Other information was imparted to John by angels, that we are not including in this study, as the study of Revelation is provided in many other books.

Suffice it to say that God's angels have been very active in past ages, are active in our day, and will be active on into the future. It is amazing to read in the Bible that many of the angels are not informed concerning God's Grand Redemptive Design, as they have continued faithful and have not needed redemption.

The Lord says: "Unto whom it was revealed, that not unto themselves, but unto us they did minister the things, which are now reported unto you by them that have preached the gospel unto you with the Holy Ghost sent down from heaven; which things the ANGELS DESIRE TO LOOK INTO" (1 Peter 1:12).

ILLUSTRATION: Is sight the real test? After listening to a Gospel address, an infidel requested permission to speak. Permission was granted and he spoke as follows: "Friends, I don't believe what this man has said; I don't believe in hell; I don't believe in a judgment; I don't believe in God; for I never saw one of them."

When he sat down another man arose and said: "Friends, you say there is a river not far from this place. It is untrue. You tell me there are trees and grass growing around where I am standing. That also is untrue. You say there are a great number of people standing here. Again I say that is not true. There is no one here except myself. I suppose you wonder what I am talking about, but I was born blind; I never saw one of you; and while I talk, it only shows that I am blind, or I would not say such things. And you," he said, turning to the infidel, "the more you talk, the more you expose your ignorance, because you are spiritually blind. Pray that your eyes may be opened" (*Prophetic News*).

There is one thing worse than being spiritually blind and ignorant, and that is to choose to be ignorant concerning the will and Word of God, when all genuine evidence proves that God is, and that He is a rewarder of those who diligently seek HIM.

Why do men choose to gamble with their never-dying souls, when Jesus who is the true source of Truth, and the Light of the world, is stretching forth His hands to rescue perishing souls from a never-ending hell and lake of fire?

His gracious invitation has been ringing down through the corridors of time, when He said, "Come unto Me, all ye that labor and are heavy laden, and I will give you rest" (Matt.11:28). As our Lord hung suspended upon the cruel cross, and said: "IT IS FINISHED!" the sins of all mankind, past, present, and future, were fully atoned for, but we must accept our pardon and salvation, by faith, and serve and worship our God. Why not trust HIM?

Appendix A.

Supplementary Questions and Answers

QUESTION: If God created the different orders of angels, male and female, similar to the creation of man, why did He not provide us with more information on the subject?

ANSWER: The Bible is a book of redemption, provided for the human family, from the time of man's creation until the consummation of all things, as they relate to man since the hour of his fall. God did not go into detail concerning all things that have transpired in His kingdom for the past millions of years, for that information is not essential to our salvation.

He also requires that we accept His Word by faith, and trust Him to impart perfect understanding when we enter His eternal, literal kingdom, after the cancellation of all temporary things.

QUESTION: Why do you think God created some angels with six wings, namely the Seraphim; the Cherubims with two wings, and some angels with no wings?

ANSWER: Why don't you ask the Lord that question when you see Him? We know the Lord loves variety, and he has provided vast evidence of that throughout all of the realm of nature. We know also that angels without wings are so similar to humans that they cannot be distinguished apart. John bowed down to a person whom he believed to be an angel, and learned that it was a human, a prophet. The Bible tells us:

"And I John saw these things, and heard them. And when I had heard and seen, I fell down to worship before the feet of the angel which showed me these things.

"Then saith he unto me, see thou do it not: for I am thy fellow servant, and of thy brethren the prophets, and of them which keep the sayings of this book: worship GOD" (Rev. 22:8,9).

QUESTION: Will some of God's angels also serve as kings and rulers in God's eternally expanding kingdom?

ANSWER: Yes, it is highly probable. Even as Lucifer reigned over nations of angelic subjects in the past eternity. The Bible tells us.

"To me, the very least of all saints, this grace was given, to preach to the Gentiles the unfathomable riches of Christ, And to bring to light what is the administration of the mystery which for ages has been hidden in God, who created all things;

In order that the manifold wisdom of God might now be known through the church to the RULERS and the AUTHORITIES in the heavenly places." (Eph. 3:8–10 NMSV).

QUESTION: Did I understand you to say that you, personally, believe that angels, in their different orders, have been multiplying gradually, since their creation perhaps millions of years ago?

ANSWER: Yes. I believe that because there is more scriptural evidence to prove that than to prove that angels are either all male or sexless.

There is ample evidence to prove, from the Bible, that the redeemed, immortal human race, will be productive, eternally, as God planned from the beginning, although there will be very little pain related to childbirth, and it will be impossible for immortal women to conceive so frequently. The curse God put upon women will be lifted.

Jesus said His redeemed people will be like the angels. In so saying He implied that angels will be like God's immortal, human saints. In plain words, there will be no difference. So, we may successfully conclude that God's immortal sons and daughters of God will provide our heavenly Father with an increasing population, eternally, in the likeness of His Son, Jesus, God the Son. Can you believe it?

We will know all things when we are ushered out into that glorious future life. If I am in error, in any area of my thinking, and teaching, I will apologize, in all humility, when we arrive in heaven.